ZEN DAWN

ZEN
DAWN

Early Zen Texts from Tun Huang

Translated by
J. C. Cleary

SHAMBHALA
Boston & London
1986

SHAMBHALA PUBLICATIONS, INC.
314 Dartmouth Street
Boston, Massachusetts 02116

© 1986 by J. C. Cleary
All rights reserved
9 8 7 6 5 4 3 2 1
First Edition
Printed in the United States of America
Distributed in the United States by Random House
and in Canada by Random House of Canada Ltd.

Library of Congress Cataloging-in-Publication Data
Main entry under title:

Zen dawn.

    1. Zen Buddhism—Doctrines—Early works to 1800.
2. Meditation (Zen Buddhism)—Early works to 1800.
I. Cleary, J. C. (Jonathan Christopher)
BQ9268.Z46 1986   294.3'927   85-27904
ISBN 0-87773-359-7 (pbk.)
ISBN 0-394-74388-1 (Random House: pbk.)

Design/Dede Cummings
Cover Illustration/Nan Starr

CONTENTS

ZEN DAWN

INTRODUCTION

THE THREE MEDITATION manuals translated in
this volume are among the earliest surviving records of
Zen (Chan) Buddhism in China. Long in oblivion in
China itself, these three texts were rediscovered in the
twentieth century among the records of Tang civilization
preserved at Tun Huang in western China.

These texts date from the first half of the eighth century, considerably earlier than the great outpouring of
Zen writings over the next five centuries in China. They
are important as historical sources because they give a
perspective on the early history of Zen that is somewhat
different from the account that became standard in the
later tradition. They are valuable Zen sources because
they preserve a record of Zen method—the theoretical
analyses and practical techniques advanced by the Zen
teachers of the time.

When we read these early Zen texts in conjunction

with the better-known records of Chinese Zen composed later, two majors points are clear. First, Zen shares the same outlook and the same intent as the Great Vehicle Buddhism of the *sūtras* and *śāstras*. Both these early texts and the later Zen tradition amply illustrate and explicitly affirm this fact: Zen teachers are shown freely quoting the *sūtras* and *śāstras*, and teaching by carrying out their theories and methods in everyday life. Second, these early texts are from the "northern school" of Zen, but in substance and even tone the Zen they show is fully in accord with the Zen of the "southern school," which shaped the later record. In the teachings of the core teachers, there is no question of sloganizing or one-sided allegiance to any one "philosophical position"—this would violate the fundamental norms of how the Buddhist teaching should be carried on.

These two points will come as no surprise to people familiar with Zen Buddhism in primary sources. They will have encountered some of the many detailed and explicit statements from within the tradition pointing out that Zen is founded on the same intent as the scriptures and cannot be at odds with them, whatever the surface appearance. Likewise, many adept teachers emphasized that the division into northern and southern schools is no essential part of Zen, and that sectarian attitudes spring from misunderstanding of the work of Zen teachers.

Nevertheless, many treatments of Buddhist history have taken for granted the notion that Buddhism can be interpreted best in terms of sectarian rivalry. Particular Buddhist doctrines are thus seen as tools devised for polemic purposes, or as ideological statements tailored to attract patronage and popularity. The flourishing of a religious school is equated with its winning support and prestige among the social elite, and the loss of such patronage is thought to mean the eclipse of the teaching. To serve this type of interpretation, texts are quoted in a fragmentary manner to show their supposed philosophical tenets, but their comprehensive meaning is studiously ignored. In particular, the message the primary sources give concerning the human realities of Buddhism is not heeded.

The result can only be pseudohistory, crippled by basic errors of method. Rather than derive from the sources an adequate paradigm for the human dimensions of Buddhist history, this type of approach simply transposes onto Buddhist history the set of human motivations and the limited range of human experiences considered normal or possible in our "modern world." As a consequence of such arbitrary presuppositions, the main factors seen at work in the formulation of Buddhist teachings are things like personal ambition and rivalry, greed for patronage, political intrigues, propaganda contests, and ideological manipulation and self-delusion through myth and fantasy. Filtered through such limiting preconceptions, which elevate the mere common sense of today's world to a universal, objective standpoint, the vision of the intent and manner of operation of the Buddhist teaching preserved in the primary sources completely escapes from view.

If we seek the social history of Buddhism in the primary sources, we find many comments from the leading Buddhist teachers through the ages from which we can derive valuable information on the sociological and psychological dimensions of Buddhism as a human phenomenon. There are descriptions of the typical states of mind of contemporary people, of the good and bad motivations that lead people to Buddhism, and of the common obstacles they encounter in remolding their customary habits and perceptions. There are discussions of the imperatives of the true teaching and the demands it makes of teachers and students. There are analyses of the distortions that crop up around Buddhism, the misconceptions and pious mystifications that block the path. And records of the great teachers provide samples of the Buddhist teaching as it was carried on. By taking careful note of all this information, we can arrive at a more adequate conceptual framework for understanding Buddhist history in human terms.

The first point to notice is that Buddhist teachings are intended as skillful, expedient means, devised and used according to the varying needs of particular audiences and situations. Religious utterances are not meant as dogmatic statements, because the truth is not seen as something that can be defined conceptually or captured in a string of words. Rather, different formulations of Buddhism are meant to have instrumental value in promoting the development of enlightened perception among those to whom the teachings are addressed. Therefore, according to its own view of religious teaching, Buddhism is naturally and properly multiform: there is no fixed doctrine. As the Zen saying goes, "If we expounded the Dharma the same way all the time, the weeds in front of the teaching hall would be ten feet deep." Teaching Buddhism is likened to curing diseases—just as there are many diseases, there are also many medicines. The enlightened teacher is like a good doctor, able to diagnose diseases and prescribe medicines accordingly.

We find that when Buddhist teachers built up conceptual structures marking out the path for students, they did not always aim for static structures, but rather aimed for subtly moving semantic devices designed to interact with and modify the students' conceptual and motivational patterns. This is especially apparent in Zen, but also present in vast creations like the *Huayan* (or *Flower Ornament*) *Sūtra* and the *Lotus Sūtra*. For thought systems like these, it is impossible to give a brief summary in terms of a few "philosophical positions" expressed in short phrases: the real semantics are not that simple. It follows that an "intellectual history" of Buddhism constructed out of such philosophical summaries cannot be true to its subject matter.

Buddhist theory has very exacting requirements for bona fide religious teachers. Real teachers must have their own independent realizations of enlightened perception, plus a thorough mastery of the full range of teaching methods known as the Buddha Dharma. Such teachers form the core of Buddhism as it is active in the world: they devise and propagate the specific adaptations of the Buddhist teaching required in their own times and places. No matter how faithful to a former master's great legacy, or how pious, rote repetition of previous methods and dogmatic allegiance to provisional doctrines cannot keep Buddhism alive.

This notion of the true teacher suggests a core and

periphery model for the social history of Buddhism. The core of enlightened teachers is the key to the real vitality of the religion. Their direct transformative influence and the influence of their teaching devices spread out into society with varying impact. Those close to the teachers may be enlightened with their help and acquire the ability to act as teachers themselves. Others near the core may be transformed enough short of enlightenment that they can serve as conduits through whom the teaching can be disseminated more widely without distortion. Others more distant from the core mentality may be emotionally inspired by the enlightened teachers and conceive feelings of respect and awe and partisan allegiance —some may become imitators or advocates of what they take to be the great teacher's message. Those around the periphery of the ring of influences emanating from the core teachers may be reached only weakly and indirectly, as their teachings have indirect effect on culture and customs. The surviving records of Buddhism contain instances of all these possibilities.

Since Buddhism operated in the ordinary world, it was unavoidably surrounded by worldly attitudes and motivations, including partisanship, jealousy, dogmatism, group rivalries, and political entanglements. The core teachers over the centuries provided penetrating analyses of the way such tendencies distorted Buddhism and blocked people from taking the Buddhist path. If we accept the core view of what Buddhism is all about, we must interpret these "all too human" phenomena as distorting influences on the periphery of the true teaching. Indeed, enlightened teachers are necessary precisely in order to counteract these ever-present tendencies toward fossilization and rote allegiance.

It follows from these considerations that no adequate account of Buddhist history can focus exclusively on peripheral phenomena while ignoring or glossing over the core teachings. The historian must therefore be familiar with the core message as well as the sociology, psychology, and cultural tradition of the periphery. This requirement means that the texts that remain as records of the teaching must be studied and understood as wholes, and in terms of their own logic, not just skimmed to cull out key phrases that are supposed to represent philosophical tenets. A history true to the human reality of Buddhism must recognize the central role of the core teachers and proceed to trace their relations to and impact on the various regions of the periphery.

For the history of early Zen in China, we are fortunate to have an account that does respect the core intent of Buddhism, while explaining the current situation of partisan disputes among the followers of the various Zen schools of the day. This is the "General Preface to Collected Explanations of the Zen Source" by Zong Mi (780–841), a Zen master also recognized as the fifth patriarch of Huayan Buddhism in China. Those scholars who insist that partisan rivalry and doctrinal differences over sudden versus gradual enlightenment were central factors in the formulation of early Zen teachings are in effect taking the position that they have a deeper insight into or better information about eighth-century Zen than Zong Mi did—a very dubious claim.

Zong Mi's account allows us to assess the true significance of the differences in early Zen between northern and southern schools and gradual and sudden conceptions of enlightenment. Pei Xiu, the ninth-century Tang official who was also a Zen adept, describes the problem Zong Mi meant to address:

> Ever since the Tathāgata appeared in the world and established teachings, and bodhisattvas went among beings pointing out medicines according to the disease, in the teachings of each era multiple methods have been developed varying in shallowness and depth. The One True Pure Mind sets forth different teachings regarding inherent nature and forms. . . .
>
> [Here Pei Xiu mentions Yogacara and Madhyamika, Tiantai, and the Zen schools of Huineng and Shenxiu, of Shenhui and Mazu, and of Oxhead Mountain.]
>
> Thus in India and China the schools of Buddhism have indeed been many and variegated: since diseases have a thousand sources, medicine comes in many kinds. [When real teachers teach] they accord with people's potentials and adapt to their capacities—they cannot be the same all the time. Nevertheless, all are gates to enlightenment, all are correct paths.
>
> But among the followers of the various schools, those who comprehend this are few, while those who are limited [to a particular formulation] are many. Thus, for the last several decades, the Teaching has been going to ruin. [Pupils] take what they have received from their teachers as signboards with which they advertise themselves. They take written teachings as spears and shields and attack each other, their sentiments varying according to whether they are attacking or defending. Teachings are considered high or low depending on whether they are one's own or someone else's. Right and wrong

are confused and made complicated, and no one can tell them apart. Thus, the various teachings of the buddhas and bodhisattvas of the past are now used to create controversy. Latter-day people are adding to the affliction and disease—how can this be beneficial?

[Zong Mi] the Great Teacher of Guifeng, having long lamented this, said: "At such a time as this I should not be silent."¹

Zong Mi gives a comprehensive account of contemporary Zen, proceeding from basic principles to a discussion of the differences among the various schools of the day. Here we can only note a few of his salient points.

Zong Mi takes as a basic fact the unity of purpose of Zen and the scriptural teachings of Buddhism. Both have their source in the fundamentally enlightened true nature of all sentient beings, also known as buddha-nature and the mind-ground.² Both have as their purpose the "one great matter" indicated in the *Lotus Sūtra* (which Zong Mi quotes): "to enable sentient beings to open up their enlightened perception."³ Zong Mi insists that the methods of cultivation and realization set forth in the scriptural teachings are basic to Zen, just as the enlightened mind of Zen is the basic intent of the *sūtras* and *śāstras*: thus, there can be no contradiction between them.⁴

With the Buddhist scriptures already in existence, why did Zen arise? "Bodhidharma received the Dharma in India and personally came to China. He saw that here students often did not get the Dharma, but instead considered naming and categorizing as understanding and formalism as practice. He wanted to let them know that the moon is not the pointing finger and that the Dharma is our own Mind."⁵ Bodhidharma stressed mind-to-mind transmission without words in order to break attachments to verbal formulations—not to reject the scriptural teachings.⁶

Zong Mi laments that many would-be Buddhists in his day fail to see the compatability between Zen and the scriptures, and use one to reject the other. "These days disciples are deluded about their source. Those who cultivate mind think the *sūtras* and *śāstras* are a different school. Those who expound the scriptures think Zen is a different teaching."⁷ "These days many Zen people do not know the meanings [of the scriptural teachings], so they just hail mind as Zen. Many who lecture on the scriptures do not know the Dharma, so they just explain the meanings according to the words. Following the names to engender clinging makes comprehensive understanding impossible."⁸ "Originally Buddha expounded sudden and gradual scriptures and Zen opened sudden and gradual gates: the two kinds of scriptures and the two kinds of gates matched and tallied with each other. But today specialists in the scriptures one-sidedly promote the gradual meaning, while Zen people one-sidedly propagate the sudden school."⁹ In this fashion, both parties go wrong: "One must know the provisional and the real in the *sūtras* and *śāstras*: only then can one distinguish right and wrong in Zen. One must recognize the real identity of Zen mind: only then can one understand the principles and events in the *sūtras* and *śāstras*."¹⁰

Zong Mi describes Zen in his day in terms of ten houses distributed across the various regions of China, teaching Zen with differing emphasis and formulations.[11]

> None of them is wrong—but since each in partisan fashion considers itself to be right and repudiates the others as wrong, it is necessary to reconcile them. . . . the Ultimate Path goes back to one pure truth, not two. . . . The Ultimate Path is not one-sided, the Final Truth is not biased. We must not seize upon the views of just one of these approaches. Thus we must understand them as one and make them all perfect and wondrous. . . . For each of them we keep what is the Dharma and get rid of the defects—then all are subtle and wondrous. . . . Many people follow sentiments and cling to one while opposing the others. . . . In essence, if you are confined to one of them, they are all wrong; if you reconcile them, they are all correct. . . . Forget sentiments and return to the ocean of wisdom.[12]

Zong Mi adopts this method himself regarding the "northern" and "southern" schools of Zen: "In the reconciliation given here, not only are sudden and gradual not opposed to each other—on the contrary, they mutually support each other."[13] Zong Mi accepts both Shenxiu (the Sixth Patriarch according to the "northern" school) and Huineng (the Sixth Patriarch according to the "southern" tradition) as true successors of Hongren, whom both schools regarded as the Fifth Zen Patriarch. Differences in teaching methods among geniune teachers Zong Mi attributes to the need to prescribe different medicines for different sicknesses. "They are just treatments according to the disease: it is not necessary to extol one and denigrate the other."[14] When Shenhui came to the capital as a proponent of Huineng's "southern" Zen and criticized the current methods of "northern" Zen, the aim was to combat issues and misapplications, not to reject legitimate methods taught by Hongren.[15]

Sectarian feeling arises among those who fail to comprehend the underlying complementarity of the sudden and gradual accounts of enlightenment. Half-baked teachers feed on and promote partisan rivalries.

> Those whose nature is superficial and shallow think themselves sufficiently equipped as soon as they hear one of these meanings. They go on to be people's teachers relying on this petty "wisdom" of theirs. Not having fully fathomed [the Buddha Dharma] from the root to the branch tips, they form many one-sided clingings. That's why followers of sudden and gradual view each other as enemies, and the northern and southern schools oppose each other like rival kingdoms.[16]

When we as modern readers come to study these long-lost early Zen texts and try to appreciate their significance, we would do well to heed these pointers offered by Zong Mi. When we compare these early works to the later, better-known records of Zen, we should follow Zong Mi's advice to "see the differences in the sameness and see the sameness in the differences."[17] Otherwise, if all we do is search for evidence of supposed sectarian rivalries, and labor to piece together questionable hypotheses about long-forgotten controversies among the ill-informed, we are using a conceptual sieve that keeps the chaff and discards the grain.

NOTES

These are page references to the "General Preface to Collected Explanations of the Zen Source," *Chan yuan zhu quan ji du xu,* No. 2015 in the Taishō Canon.

1.	398bc.	10.	400b.
2.	399ab.	11.	400c.
3.	408b.	12.	400c.
4.	400b.	13.	402a.
5.	400b.	14.	404a.
6.	400b.	15.	405b.
7.	400b.	16.	402b.
8.	401c.	17.	410c.
9.	399c.		

Records of the Teachers and Students of the Lanka

ORIGINAL PREFACE

[TEXT BROKEN OFF] . . . It was evident that the Great Teacher [Xuanze] had long since consummated the Path. In 708 he was called by imperial summons to the Western Capital; he preached the methods of Chan widely in the Eastern Capital.

[I,] Jingjue was in his assembly and took refuge with him, serving him single-mindedly. I traveled back and forth between the two capitals, studying earnestly with him: the mental states that had appeared [in me] over the past several years were soon resolved.

Among those to whom the Great Teacher Hongren had given predictions [of enlightenment], there was one from Anzhou—this was my great teacher [Xuanze]. In appearance he was like an ordinary monk, but in his realization he shared the stage of the buddhas. He was the imperial teacher, a national treasure to whom people throughout the land gave their allegiance. Since I had a causal link with him from past lives, I personally received his instructions: only then did I come to know that the inner heart is fully endowed with True Thusness. Things I had never before heard I now found out.

True Thusness has no form; knowledge [of it] is without knowing. Knowledge without knowing—could it be apart from knowing? Form without form—could it be apart from form? Human beings and phenomena are all Thus; speaking, too, is Thus. Thusness of itself is without speech; with speech, it is not Thusness. Thusness basically is without knowing; with knowing, it is not Thusness. The *Awakening of Faith Treatise* says: "The True Thusness of Mind is the comprehensive aspect of the One Reality, the essential body of the Dharma Gate."

What is called the reality-nature of mind is neither born nor destroyed. There are distinctions among all phenomena only based on false thoughts. The forms of objects do not exist separately apart from the mind's thoughts. Therefore, from the beginning, all things are detached from the forms of language, detached from the forms of names, and detached from the forms of mental objects: they are ultimately equal, without change, and indestructible: they are just the One Mind. Hence the name True Thusness.

Moreover, the inherent essential being of True Thusness is neither augmented nor diminished in ordinary people, *śrāvaka*s, bodhisattvas, or buddhas. It is neither born in the past nor destroyed in the future: ultimately, it endures forever. From its fundamental nature it is self-sufficient in all virtues. In its own essential being it has the light of great wisdom: thus, it is the pure mind of inherent reality.

The *Laṅkāvatāra Sūtra* says: "Inherent Mind manifests objects appearing everywhere amid the five phenomena according to kind." What are the five phenomena? Names, forms, false thinking, true wisdom, and thusness. For this reason, all things are nameless: they are named by mind. All forms are formless: they are given form by mind. Just be mindless oneself, and there are no names or forms. Then it is called true wisdom and thusness. The *Dharmapada Sūtra* says: "The dense array of myriad images is the impression of One Reality."

So I immersed my spirit in dark silence, and nurtured my real identity on remote cliffsides, holding solely to the mind of purity, preserving oneness until it filled the valleys. Composing a preface, I lodge my enlightenment within it, in the hope that those who share in the stream of our Path will come to know Mind. The wondrous essence of True Thusness is not apart from birth and death. The abstruse subtlety of the Path of the Sages lies within the body of form. The purity of the body of form is lodged amid afflictions. The inherent reality of birth and death is provisionally located in *nirvāna*.

Thus we know that sentient beings and buddha-nature share a common identity. They are like water and ice—what difference is there in their essential being? The solid barrier of ice represents the bondage of sentient beings. Water by nature energizes and flows through: it is equivalent to the perfect purity of buddha-nature.

There is nothing that can be attained, no form that can

be sought. Even good things are dispensed with, so birth and death must be left far behind.

The *Vimalakīrti Sūtra* says: "If one would attain the perfection of purity, one must purify one's mind. As one's mind is purified, so the buddha-land is purified." Though physical existence is the basis for them, consciousness and perception range from shallow to deep. As for profound perceptions, they are pure through the ages—they are the basis to influence and cultivate [mind] from the first generation of the aspiration for enlightenment until the achievement of buddhahood without falling back. As for shallow consciousness, this is what new students today have—although they are delighted at the outset, they lack the power to practice the Path with correct faith, owing to slanderous and twisted views accumulated for lifetimes. Since the basis is not firm, later they fall back in defeat.

Repeatedly undergoing birth and death is just due to grasping at objects. When we reflect back on the mind that grasps at objects, [we see] that the real identity of mind is originally pure. Within this purity, [grasping] mind really does not exist. Within the peaceful extinction [of *nirvāṇa*], fundamentally there are no thoughts moving: the movement is ever still. Being still, there is no seeking. Where the thoughts are is ever real. Being real, there are no defilements or attachments. Having no defilements is purity. Having no bonds is liberation. Defilement is the basis of birth and death. Purity is the fruit of enlightenment.

Even profound concepts are ultimately empty: the Ultimate Path is wordless, and if we speak, we go away

from it. Though we may characterize the fundamental
basis as "empty by nature," there is no "fundamental
basis" that can be labeled. Emptiness itself is wordless: it
is not a mental construct. The Mind of the Sages is
subtle, hidden, beyond understanding and knowing.
Great Enlightenment is dark and mysterious, wordless
and speechless. The *Lotus Sūtra* says: "The *nirvāṇa* aspect
of all phenomena cannot be communicated verbally."

There is no Dharma that can be explained, no Mind
that can be spoken of: inherent reality-nature is empty.
Going back to the fundamental basis, it is the Path. The
real identity of the Path is empty and boundless, vast and
pure. With its stillness and solitude, it obliterates the
cosmos. It pervades ancient and modern, but its nature
is pure. It is perfect from top to bottom and everywhere
pure. This is the pure buddha-land.

Thus we know that within a single hair the whole
universe is fully present; within an atom of dust are
contained boundless worlds. These words have true substance: those who meditate on this and witness it will
know for themselves, not follow what is explained by the
Three Vehicles.

A *sūtra* says: "The Path of enlightenment cannot be
charted or measured: highest of the high, vast beyond
limit, deepest of the deep, profound beyond fathoming,
big enough to contain heaven and earth, small enough to
enter an infinitesimal point—thus it is called the Path."

Therefore, the body of reality is pure as empty space.
But emptiness is not empty and existence does not exist.
Existence basically does not exist—people themselves be-
come attached to existence. Emptiness is basically not

empty—people themselves become attached to emptiness. Pure liberation is apart from existence and emptiness, without contrived actions, without concerns,
without abiding, without attachment. Within *nirvāṇa*,
not a single thing is created. This is the contemplation of
enlightenment.

Thus the fruit of the Path of *nirvāṇa* does not lie
within being and nothingness, nor is it beyond being and
nothingness. This being so, the people who enter the
Path do not abolish existence or nonexistence: the forms
and methods they uphold are just provisional devices.
Therefore, essence is empty and formless, so it cannot be
considered existent; function is not abrogated, so it cannot be considered nonexistent. Empty, it always functions; functioning, it is always empty. Though the
emptiness and the functioning are distinct, there is no
mind to consider them different. This is True Thusness,
pure by nature, eternally abiding and undestroyed.

I sigh and say: There are those in the world who do
not know how to cultivate the Path; they are tied down
by being and nothingness. Being does not exist by itself:
before the causal nexus is born, it does not exist. Nothingness is not nonexistent by itself: it is nonexistent because the causal nexus has dispersed. If being
fundamentally existed, it would exist externally of itself:
it would not wait for the causal nexus to exist. If nothingness were fundamentally nonexistent, it would be externally nonexistent of itself: it would not wait for the causal
nexus to end to be nonexistent. Seeming existence does
not exist: within True Thusness there are no self-existent
objects. Nothingness is not nothingness: within Pure

Mind there is no such nothingness. The phenomena "being" and "nothingness" are in the realm of false conceptions. How could they be adequate to represent the Path of the Sages?

The *Light-Emitting Perfection of Wisdom Sūtra* says: "Is enlightenment attained from being? No. Is it attained from nothingness? No. Is it attained from being and nothingness? No. Is it attained apart from being and nothingness? No. What does this mean? There is nothing attained. Attaining without attainment is called attaining enlightenment."

❧

SECTION ONE

Gunabhadra of the Song Period

Gunabhadra Tripitaka was a man of South India. When he studied the Great Vehicle, he was called "Mahayana." During the Yuan Jia years (424–454) he came by ship to Guangzhou. Emperor Taizu of the Song received him at Danyang Commandery. He translated the *Laṅkāvatāra Sūtra*. Princes and nobles, monks and laymen, invited him to give instructions on meditation, but Gunabhadra was embarrassed [and declined] because he did not speak Chinese well. That night he dreamed that a man took off his head with a sword: thenceforth he began to give lessons on meditation.

Gunabhadra said: This country is located in the East

[25]

and lacks methods of cultivating the Path. Since they lack such methods, some fall into the teachings of the Lesser Vehicle and the Two Vehicles; some fall into the teachings of the ninety-five kinds of outside paths; some fall into demonic meditation, in order to view all things and find out the good and bad deeds of other people. How bitter! What a great misfortune! They entrap themselves and entrap others. I feel sorry for these types, who fall for long ages into demonic paths subject to birth and death, and do not attain liberation. Some fall into forbidden magical arts, controlling spirits and demons, spying on other people's good and bad deeds: they falsely say, "I sit in meditation and practice contemplation." Ordinary people are blind and deluded and do not understand, and think that [such magicians] have indeed realized the Path of the Sages, and submit to them. They do not know that these are perverse, demonic methods.

In our land we have the Correct Teaching, but it is secret and not openly transmitted. Those who have an affinity with it and whose faculties are fully prepared meet good and wise men on the road who bestow it on them. If not for encounters with good and wise teachers, there would be no transmission from "father" to "son."

The *Laṅkāvatāra Sūtra* says: "The Mind of the buddhas is supreme: when the Dharma is bestowed in our teaching, where [deluded] states of mind do not arise, it is this." This Dharma surpasses the Three Vehicles and goes beyond the ten stages. Ultimately the fruit of enlightenment can only be known for oneself with mind silent. Mindless, we nurture the spirit; without thought, we pacify the body. Without preoccupations, we sit in purity, preserving the fundamental and returning to the real. Our Dharma is secret and silent; it is not transmitted by common fools of shallow consciousness. Only people rich in merit and virtue can receive it and carry it out.

If you do not understand, if you are not liberated, the sixth [consciousness] possesses the seventh and the eighth. If you do understand, if you are liberated, the eighth [consciousness] is without the sixth and seventh.

Those who intend to be buddhas should first learn to pacify mind. Before mind is pacified, even good things are not good—so much the worse for evil. When mind becomes peaceful and still, neither good nor evil has any basis. The *Huayan Sūtra* says: "Phenomena do not see each other, phenomena do not know each other."

Since coming to this country, I have not even seen people who cultivate the Path, much less anyone who has pacified mind. I often see people who go along creating *karma*, who have not merged with the Path. Some are concerned with fame and reputation; some act for the sake of profit and support. They operate with the mentality of self and others; they act with the attitude of jealousy. What is jealousy? It means to engender the mentality of resentment and hatred when you see someone else cultivating the Path and reaching consummation in principle and practice, so that many people offer support and give their allegiance. It means self-satisfied reliance on your own intelligence, not using it to overcome self—this is called jealousy. Even if you scrupulously perform various practices day and night, cut off afflictions and clear away obstructions, with this kind of attitude, barriers to the Path arise one after another, and you do not find peace and stillness. This is just called "cultivating the Path"; it is not called "pacifying mind."

Even if you practice the six *pāramitā*s, expound the scriptures, sit in meditation, and advance energetically practicing austerities, this is just called "being good"; it is not called "Dharma practice." If you do not irrigate the karmic field with the water of desire, if you do not plant the seeds of consciousness there, this is called "Dharma practice."

Just now I spoke of pacifying mind. In brief, there are four kinds of mentality. First, the mentality that turns away from truth: this is the mentality of those who go through life as ordinary people. Second, the mentality that turns toward truth: this means loathing birth and death and so seeking *nirvāṇa* and going toward stillness: it is called the *śrāvaka* mentality. Third, the mind that enters truth: though you cut off barriers [to the Path] and reveal inner truth, subject and object are not yet nullified: this is the bodhisattva mentality. Fourth, the mind of truth: not mind outside truth, not truth outside mind; truth *is* mind. Mind is able to be everywhere equal, so it is called truth. Truth's awareness can illuminate everything, so it is called mind. Mind and truth are everywhere equal, so it is called buddha-mind, the mind of enlightenment.

Those who understand reality do not see any difference between birth and death and *nirvāṇa* or ordinary and holy. Objects and knowledge are not two: inner truth and phenomena are fused. Real and conventional are viewed as equal; defilement and purity are one Suchness.

Buddhas and sentient beings are fundamentally equal and at one.

The *Laṅkāvatāra Sūtra* says: "There is no *nirvāṇa* in anything: no *nirvāṇa-buddha*, no *buddha-nirvāṇa*. It is detached from awakening and that which is awakened to, detached from both being and nothingness." The Great Path is fundamentally omnipresent, perfectly pure, and basically existent: it is not attained from causes. It is like the sun hidden behind floating clouds: when the clouds are gone, the sun appears by itself. What's the use of any more learning or views? Why become involved in written or spoken words, and come back again to the path of birth and death? Those who take verbal explanations and literary accounts as the Path covet fame and profit: they ruin themselves and ruin others. It is like polishing a mirror: when the dust on the surface has been totally removed, the mirror of itself is bright and clear.

All things are uncompounded. The *sūtra* says: "The Buddha is not Buddha, nor does he save sentient beings. Sentient beings impose distinctions, and think that Buddha saves sentient beings: thus they do not realize this Mind, and they have no stability." With realization, there is awareness, and Great Function amid causal origination, penetrating perfectly without obstruction: this is called "Great Cultivation of the Path." There is no duality between self and other. All practices are carried out at once: there is no before or after, and no in between. It is called the Great Vehicle.

Having no attachments within or without, the great ultimate relinquishment—this is called *dānapāramitā*, the perfection of giving. Good and evil equal, so neither can be found—this is *śīlapāramitā*, the perfection of morality. To have no transgressions amid the objects of mind, the harm of rancor forever ended—this is *kṣāntipāramitā*, the perfection of patience. Great stillness unmoving, the myriad activities spontaneously so—this is *vīryapāramitā*, the perfection of energetic progress. The flourishing of wondrous stillness—this is *dhyānapāramitā*, the perfection of meditation. Wondrous stillness opening forth illumination—this is *prajñāpāramitā*, the perfection of wisdom. People who are like this are lofty and vast, taking in everything perfectly without obstruction, achieving rich and varied functioning. This is the Great Vehicle.

If they do not first learn to pacify mind, those who seek the Great Vehicle are sure to err in their knowledge. The *Mahāprajñāpāramitā Sūtra* says: "The five eyes of the buddhas observe the minds of sentient beings and all phenomena ultimately without seeing." The *Huayan Sūtra* says: "If you have no views, then you can see." The *Si Yi Sūtra* says: "It is not something seen with the eyes or known by the senses. It must be seen by according with Thusness. All the senses are Thus, and so is the Thusness of the Dharma. Seeing like this is called correct seeing." The *Chan Jue* says: "Bats and owls do not see things in daylight, but rather by night. This is due to the inversions of false thinking. How so? Bats and owls see what to others is darkness as light. Ordinary people see what to others is light as darkness. Both are cases of false thinking. Because of their inverted perceptions, because of their karmic barriers, [ordinary people] do not see reality. This being so, light is not definitely light and darkness is not definitely darkness. If you understand like this, and you are not confused by inverted thinking, then you will enter into the eternity, the bliss, the personality, and the purity of the *tathāgata*s."

The Great Teacher [Gunabhadra] said: "The *Laṅkā-vatāra Sūtra* says: 'How can one purify one's thoughts? Do not allow false thinking. Do not allow defiled thinking. Put your utmost energy into mindfulness of buddha. Let mindfulness of buddha continue without a break: you will be still, without thoughts, and you will witness the fundamental empty purity.'" He also said: "Once this is received, you do not fall back from eternal stillness. Thus Buddha said, 'How can it be increased?'" He also said: "You learn from the teacher, but enlightenment does not come from the teacher. Whoever would 'make people wise' has never expounded the Dharma. It is verified in the event."

He also said: "Can you enter a jar? Can you enter a pillar? Can you enter fire? Can you go through a mountain? Do you enter bodily or do you enter mentally?" He also said: "In a room there is a jar. Is the jar also outside the room or not? Is there water in the jar? Is the jar in the water? Are there jars in all the waters in the world? What is this water?"

He also said: "The leaves of a tree can preach the Dharma. A jar can preach the Dharma. A pillar can preach the Dharma. A staff can preach the Dharma. A room can preach the Dharma. Earth, water, fire, and air can all preach the Dharma. Earth, wood, tile, and stone can also preach the Dharma. What is this?"

≈

SECTION TWO

Tripitaka Dharma Teacher
Bodhidharma
Wei Period

It was Meditation Master Bodhidharma who took it up
after Gunabhadra Tripitaka. Intent on clarifying the
Great Vehicle, he traveled by sea to Wu Yue [coastal
southeast China] and traveled north to Ye [the capital of
the Wei]. The monks Daoyu and Huike served him for
five years before he instructed them in the Four Practices. He said to Huike: "There is the *Laṅkāvatāra
Sūtra,* in four scrolls: if you practice according to it, you
will naturally be liberated. . ." The rest in full is as
recorded clearly in the biography in the *Continuation of
the Biographies of Eminent Monks* [by Daoxuan, d. 667]
and as outlined in his disciple Tanlin's preface to the
Four Practices for Entering the Path of the Great Vehicle.

The Dharma Teacher Bodhidharma was a man of
southern India, the third son of a local monarch. His
intellect was very incisive and clear, and he clearly
understood what he was taught. His will was set on the
Great Vehicle, so he abandoned lay life and became a
monk. He perpetuated the seed of the sages and made it
flourish. With deepest mind empty and still, he saw
through and comprehended the things and events of the
world. Inner and outer, he was clear about it all. His

[32]

virtue went beyond the world: his compassion and concern reached every corner of the land. The Correct Teaching was in decline, so he came from afar across mountains and seas, traveling to teach in the lands of China. Those who [cultivated] mind-emptied still silence all believed in him. The type who cling to forms and fixate on opinions began to slander and denounce him.

During this time he only had the two monks Daoyu and Huike with him. Though they were younger, they brought with them wills that were lofty and far-reaching. Being fortunate enough to meet with the Dharma Teacher, they served him many years, respectfully seeking instruction. They learned well, encountering the Teacher's intent. Moved by their fine energy and sincerity, the Dharma Teacher instructed them in the True Path. He taught them how to pacify mind, how to develop practice, how to accord with beings, and how to employ skill in means.

This is the Great Vehicle Teaching for pacifying mind —let there be no error. Those who pacify mind like this do wall-gazing. Those who develop practice like this do the Four Practices. Those who accord with beings like this prevent slander and dislike. Those who have skill in means like this dispense with what does not apply. Here I abbreviate what is to be followed: the message is in the text below.

[Bodhidharma taught:]

There are many roads for entering the Path, but in essence they do not go beyond two kinds: one is entering through inner truth, and the other is entering through practice.

Entering through inner truth means using the Teachings to awaken to the source. It means deep belief that living beings both ordinary and sage share one and the same reality-nature; it is just because of the false covering of alien dust that it is not manifested. If you abandon the false and return to the real, concentrate your attention and gaze like a wall, then there is no self and others, and ordinary and sage are equal. Firmly abiding and unmoving, you no longer fall into the verbal teachings. This is tacit accord with the real inner truth: without discrimination, it is still and nameless. This is called "entering through inner truth."

Entering through practice refers to the Four Practices —all other practices are contained within these. What are the Four Practices? First, the practice of repaying wrongs. Second, the practice of going along with the causal nexus. Third, the practice of not seeking anything. Fourth, the practice of according with the Dharma.

What is the practice of repaying wrongs? When receiving suffering, a practitioner who cultivates the Path should think to himself: "During countless ages past I have abandoned the root and pursued the branches, flowing into the various states of being, and giving rise to much rancor and hatred—the transgression, the harm done, has been limitless. Though I do not transgress now, this suffering is a disaster left over from former lives—the results of evil deeds have ripened. This suffering is not something given by gods or humans." You should willingly endure the suffering without anger or complaint. The *sūtra* says: "Encountering suffering, one is not concerned. Why? Because one is conscious of the basic root." When this attitude [toward suffering] is born, you are in accord with inner truth, and even as you experience wrongs, you advance on the Path. Thus it is called "the practice of repaying wrongs."

Second is the practice of going along with the causal nexus. Sentient beings have no selves, but are transformed [in a manner] causally linked to their deeds. They receive both suffering and happiness—both are born from causal conditions. If we get good rewards, glory and fame and the like, this is brought about by past causes. We receive them now, but when the causal nexus is ended, they will not be there—how can we rejoice? Gain and loss follow the causal nexus: Mind is neither augmented nor diminished. If the wind of joy [at gain and sorrow at loss] does not stir, you deeply accord with the Path. Thus it is called "the practice of going along with the causal nexus."

Third, the practice of not seeking anything. Worldly people are always deluded, craving everything, becoming attached everywhere. This is called "seeking." The wise awaken to the real. Using inner truth, they reach the conventional world. Pacifying mind without contrived activity, changing shape as they go, the myriad states of being are thereby emptied, and there is nothing wished for to take joy in. Along with this, the darkness of "meritorious deeds" [contrived based on dualistic views] is forever banished. Dwell for long in the triple world?—it is like a house on fire. All who have bodies suffer—who can find peace? When this is completely comprehended, thoughts of the various states of being cease and there is no seeking. The *sūtra* says: "All who seek, suffer. If there is no seeking, only then is there bliss." Thus we know that not seeking anything is truly a practice of the Path.

Fourth, the practice of according with the Dharma. The Dharma, the Teaching of Reality, is based on the inner truth of the inherent purity [of all things' true identity]. By this inner truth the multitude of forms are all empty: there is no defilement, no attachment, no this, no that. The *sūtra* says: "The Dharma has no sentient beings, because it is detached from the impurity of sentient beings. The Dharma has no self, because it is detached from the impurity of self." If the wise can believe and understand with certainty this inner truth, they ought to practice in accord with the Dharma. The body of the Dharma is not stingy with the physical body and life. This is practicing giving: let there be no stinginess or holding back in the heart. Realizing that the one receiving the gift, the giver, and the gift itself are all empty, you don't depend on them or get attached to them. They are just used to get rid of impurities, and embrace and transform sentient beings, without grasping at forms. This is benefiting oneself and also being able to benefit others, and being able to adorn the Path of Enlightenment. Since the perfection of giving is thus, so are the other five [the perfection of morality, patient endurance, energetic progress, meditation, and wisdom]. To practice the six perfections to remove false thinking, and yet to have nothing that is practiced—this is the practice of according with the Dharma.

These Four Practices were personally expounded by the Chan Master Bodhidharma. In addition, his disciple Tanlin recorded the Teacher's sayings and doings and collected them into a volume called the *Bodhidharma Treatise*. Bodhidharma also explained the essential meaning of the *Laṅkāvatāra Sūtra* for the communities doing sitting meditation, in twelve or thirteen pages: this, too, is called the *Bodhidharma Treatise*. Both these two works are round and full in their language and principles, and they circulate throughout the world. There were also some outsiders who forged a three-volume "Bodhidharma Treatise"—its language is prolix and its principles sloppy, and it is not fit for practical use.

The Great Teacher Bodhidharma would point to things and ask their meaning. He would just point to something—"What is it called? There is a multitude of things—question them all. Interchange their names, and with them changed, question them."

He also said: "Does this body exist or not? What body *is* this body?"

He also said: "The clouds in the sky can never stain the empty sky, but they can cover over the sky so that it is not bright and clear."

The *Nirvāṇa Sūtra* says: "Inside, there are no senses; outside, there are no sense objects. Since inner and outer align, it is called the Middle Path."

✎

SECTION THREE

Huike

A monk of the Capital in the Qi Period

The one who took it up after the Chan Master Bodhidharma was the Chan Master Huike. His lay surname was Ji, and he was from Wulao. At the age of fourteen, he met Bodhidharma, who was traveling and teaching in the region [modern Henan]. Huike served him for six years, investigating the One Vehicle with pure energy and drawing near to the abstruse inner truth.

Huike gave an outline account of cultivating the Path and of the essential method for illuminating Mind, whereby one truly reaches the fruit of enlightenment.

The *Laṅkāvatāra Sūtra* says: "Śākyamuni contemplated in stillness, and thus left birth and death far behind. This is called 'not grasping.'" Of all the enlightened ones of the ten directions, past and present, there is not one who became buddha without a basis in sitting meditation.

The *Ten Stages Sūtra* says: "Within the bodies of sentient beings there is an indestructible enlightened nature. It is like the orb of the sun: its body is bright, round, and full, [its light] vast and boundless. Because it is covered over by the layered clouds of the five *skandha*s, sentient beings do not see it. If you encounter the wind of wisdom, it blows away the five *skandha*s. When the

[38]

layers of clouds are totally gone, the enlightened nature is shining perfectly bright, clear, and pure."

The *Huayan Sūtra* says: "It is as vast as the universe, as ultimate as the void. But it is also like a light in a jar that cannot illuminate the outside." Another simile is this: When clouds close in on all sides and the world is darkened, how can the sunlight be bright and clear? The sunlight has not been destroyed—it is just covered over and blocked off by the clouds. The pure reality-nature of sentient beings is also like this. It cannot become fully manifest precisely because layers upon layers of clouds— afflictions, the perceptions of false thoughts clinging to objects—cover over and block off the Path of the Sages. If false thoughts are not born, and you sit in silent purity, the sun of great *nirvāṇa* is spontaneously bright and clear.

A worldly book says: "Ice is born from water, but ice can block water. Ice is solid, whereas water flows." [Similarly,] falsity arises from the real, and falsity can lose the real in delusion. When falsity is ended, the real appears—the mind-sea is clear and pure, the body of reality is empty and clean.

Therefore, when learners rely on written and spoken words as the Path, these are like a lamp in the wind: they cannot dispel darkness, and their flame dies away. But if learners sit in purity without concerns, it is like a lamp in a closed room: it can dispel the darkness, and it illuminates things with clarity.

If you completely comprehend the clear purity of the mind-source, then all vows are fulfilled, all practices are completed, all is accomplished. You are no longer subject to states of being. For those who find this body of reality [*dharmakāya*], the numberless sentient beings are just one good person: the one person who has been there in accord with This through a million billion aeons.

If pure energy and true integrity are not generated within you, it accomplishes nothing even if you encounter countless buddhas past, present, and future. Thus we know that sentient beings save themselves by knowing Mind—the buddhas do not save the sentient beings. If the buddhas can save sentient beings, since we have met countless buddhas in the past, why haven't we become enlightened? It is just because pure energy and integrity have not been generated within. Unless the mind attains what the mouth speaks of, you will never avoid taking on form according to your deeds.

Thus, enlightened nature is like sun and moon to the world. Within wood, there is [the potential for] fire. Within humans, there is an enlightened true identity; it is also called the lamp of buddha-nature and the mirror of *nirvāṇa*. The great *nirvāṇa* mirror is brighter than sun and moon: inside and out it is perfectly pure, boundless, and infinite.

Another simile is smelting gold. When the dross is obliterated, the pure gold is unharmed. When the forms "sentient beings" and "birth and death" are obliterated, the body of reality is unharmed.

Accomplishment in sitting meditation is experienced by oneself within one's own body. Thus a picture of a cake is not fit for a meal: if you speak of feeding it to other people, how can it satisfy them? Though you wish to remove the blockages of the past, instead you make the future offshoots even stronger. The *Huayan Sūtra* says: "It is like being a poor man, day and night counting the treasures of others without having a single penny of his own."

Being learned is also like this. Moreover, those who read should only look at books for a while, then hasten to put them away [to test them in practice]. If you do not give them up, it is the same as verbal learning—this is no different from looking for ice by boiling water.

Thus, all the verbal explanations spoken by the buddhas speak of the unspoken. Amid the reality of all phenomena, they are speechless, but nothing is left unsaid. If you understand this, when one is raised, a thousand follow. The *Lotus Sūtra* says: "Not real, not false, not thus, not otherwise."

The Great Teacher Huike said: "I explain this True Dharma as it really is: ultimately it is no different from the real, profound inner truth. [Sentient beings] mistake the wish-fulfilling jewel for tiles and pebbles. When they empty out and realize for themselves that it is a real jewel, then ignorance and wisdom are equal and no different. You must realize that the myriad phenomena are all Thus.

"Out of pity for those with dualistic views, I take up a brush and write this. When you observe that your body is no different from the Buddha's, there is no need to search further for final *nirvāṇa*."

He also said: "When I first generated the mind intent on enlightenment, I cut off one arm and stood in the snow from twilight until midnight, not noticing the snow

pile up past my knees, because I was seeking the Supreme
Path."

In the seventh scroll of the *Huayan Sūtra* it says: "Entering correct concentration in the east, *samādhi* arising
in the west. Entering correct concentration in the west,
samādhi arising in the west. Entering true concentration
in the eye, *samādhi* arising in the phenomena of form: it
reveals that the phenomena of form are inconceivable and
beyond the ken of *deva*s and humans. Entering correct
concentration in the phenomena of form, *samādhi* arising
in the eye, so that mindfulness is not disturbed. We
observe that the eye is unborn and has no inherent identity; we observe empty, still extinction without anything
at all. It is this way, too, with ear, nose, tongue, body,
and conceptual mind.

"Entering correct concentration in the body of a boy,
samādhi arising in the body of a grown man. Entering
correct concentration in the body of a grown man, *samādhi* arising in the body of an old man. Entering correct concentration in the body of an old man, *samādhi*
arising in the body of a good woman. Entering correct
concentration in the body of a good woman, *samādhi*
arising in the body of a good man. Entering correct
concentration in the body of a good man, *samādhi* arising
in the body of a nun. Entering correct concentration in
the body of a nun, *samādhi* arising in the body a monk.
Entering correct concentration in the body of a monk,
samādhi arising in the stages of study and the stages beyond study. Entering in correct concentration in the
[*śrāvaka*'s] stages of study and beyond study, *samādhi*
arising in the body of a *pratyeka* buddha. Entering cor-

rect concentration in the body of a *pratyeka, samādhi* arising in the body of a *tathāgata*. Entering correct concentration in a single pore, *samādhi* arising in all pores. Entering correct concentration in all pores, *samādhi* arising on the tip of one hair. Entering correct concentration on the tip of one hair, *samādhi* arising on the tips of all hairs. Entering correct concentration on the tips of all hairs, *samādhi* arising in an atom of dust. Entering correct concentration in an atom of dust, *samādhi* arising in all atoms of dust. Entering correct concentration in the great ocean, *samādhi* arising in the great conflagration. One body can be countless bodies, and countless bodies can be one body."

If you understand this, when one is raised, a thousand follow. The myriad things are all Thus.

☙

SECTION FOUR

Meditation Teacher Sengcan
of Sikong Mountain in Shuzhou
Sui Period

The one who took it up after the Chan Master Huike was the Chan Master Sengcan. His lay surname and his original station in life are unknown, as is his place of birth. According to the *Continuation of Biographies of Eminent Monks:*

After Huike was Chan Master Sengcan. He concealed

himself on Sikong Mountain, living in solitude, sitting in purity. He did not put any writings into circulation: he taught only intimately, at close range, and did not publicly transmit the Dharma. He had only one known disciple, the monk Daoxin, who served him for twelve years. Thus did Sengcan fashion the vessel and transmit the lamp, complete in every respect: he certified Daoxin's complete perception of buddha-nature. Sengcan told Daoxin: "The *Lotus Sūtra* says that there is just this one thing [the Buddha Vehicle, leading to the perception of buddhas]: there is really no second or third. Thus we know that the Path of the Sages is profound and pervasive, something that verbal explanations cannot reach. The body of reality is empty and still, something that seeing and hearing cannot touch. Thus written and spoken words are vain constructs."

The Great Teacher Sengcan said: "Everyone else thinks it is noble to die sitting: they sigh at such a marvel. Now I will die standing, independent of birth and death." His words finished, he held on to the branch of a tree as his breath gently ended.

He died at Nieshan Temple, where there is now an image of him. His work *Details of the Mysterious Transmission* says:

There is only the vast depths of the One Reality. Ah, for the profuse diversity of the myriad forms. True and conventional differ, but their essential body is the same. Ordinary and sage are divided, but the Path joins them. If we look for a shore, it is vast and boundless, stretching out of sight to infinity. It takes its source in the beginningless and reaches its limit in the endless. This runs through both liberation and delusion alike: both defiled and pure are fused in this. It includes emptiness and existence with perception still: it embraces space and time with pervasive sameness. It is like the pure gold that is not apart from the rings [made of it]. It is like a mass of water that does not fear surface ripples.

[Note: This explains how the inner truth is without gaps or admixtures; hence the talk of boundlessness and endlessness. Reality-nature is not a material creation. Putting to rest theories of beginning and end, he thereby explains the canceling out of light and darkness in the gate of nonduality, and the fusion of good and evil in the path of uniformity. Thus there is no motion that is not still, no difference that is not the same.]

It is like water making waves, like gold making vessels. The gold is the substance of the vessel, so no vessel is not gold. The waves are the functioning of the water, so no waves are different from the water. We observe nonobstruction amid causal origination and are certain about the inconceivability of the nature of things. It is like pearls hanging down from a jeweled palace, like mirrors hung from an agate pedestal. This and that differ, but they enter into each other. Red and purple are separate, but they reflect each other. With things we are not stuck on self and others; with events we do not weigh crooked and straight.

An infinitesimally small space contains all the phenomena of the great thousand-world system. An instant of time includes all the times of past, present, and future.

Fearing that few will believe such words, we use Indra's Net to remove doubts. The universal eye can see this, but how can deluded consciousness come to know it?

[Note: This explains the esoteric level of causal origination. In the realm of Indra's Net, one is all: they align without being the same. It is so because forms do not have their own reality, and to arise must depend on the real. Once fused in real inner truth, forms, too, have no obstructions among them.]

Though large and small differ, they are like images in a mirror that enter into each other. Though this and that differ, they are like the mutually reflected shapes of the jewels [in Indra's Net]. One thing is everything, everything is one thing. Causal origination has no obstructions: inner truth is clear in each and every thing. Thus we know that however broad the cosmos, it can fit into an atom of dust without being cramped. However long past, present, and future are, they can be contained in a brief moment. Thus we can see through metal walls, observing that there is nothing to be measured; we can pass through stone walls without any obstruction.

Thereby do the sages find inner truth and perfect their functioning. If inner truth did not let them be so, the sages would not have such power. Liberation is penetration through inner truth. Obstruction is due to blockage by sentiments. The wisdom of the universal eye can see things as they really are.

When the monkey wears chains, he stops his restless movement. When the snake enters a tube, he straightens out his curves. Cross the vast sea with the boat of discipline. Illuminate the thick darkness with the lamp of wisdom.

[Note: The monkey wearing chains is a metaphor for discipline controlling the mind. The snake entering a tube is a metaphor for concentration stopping confusion. The *Perfection of Wisdom Treatise* says: "The way a snake moves is naturally crooked, but when it enters a tube it straightens out. The way *samādhi* controls the mind is also like this." The Three Bodies Section of the *Golden Light Sūtra* says: "Though there are three names for Buddha, there are not three essences."]

≈

SECTION FIVE

Meditation Teacher Daoxin
of Shuangfeng Mountain
in Jizhou
Tang Period

The one who took it up after the Chan Master Sengcan was the Chan Master Daoxin. He opened the Chan Gate again, and it spread throughout the country. He had a volume, *Methods of Bodhisattva Discipline*, and he devised essential expedient methods for entering the Path and pacifying mind.

[Daoxin taught:] I expound this teaching of mine for those whose causal conditions and capacities are ripe for

[47]

them. You must go by the *Laṅkāvatāra Sūtra:* make the mind of the buddhas number one. And go by the one-practice *samādhi* in the *Prajñā Sūtra Spoken by Mañjuśrī.* If you are mindful of the buddha-mind, you are a buddha; if you have false mindfulness, then you are an ordinary person. In the *Prajñā Sūtra Spoken by Mañjuśrī* it says: "Mañjuśrī said, 'World Honored One, what is one-practice *samādhi?*' Buddha said, 'Being linked to the realm of reality through its oneness is called one-practice *samādhi.*' If men and women want to enter one-practice *samādhi,* first they must learn about *prajñāpāramitā* and cultivate their learning accordingly. Later they will be capable of one-practice *samādhi* and, if they do not retreat from or spoil their link with the realm of reality, of inconceivable unobstructed formlessness.

"Good men and good women, if you want to enter one-practice *samādhi,* you must be empty and at ease, and abandon all confused ideas. Not grasping at forms and appearances, you bind your heart to one Buddha, and concentrate on invoking his name. Wherever the Buddha may be, straighten your body and face toward him. If you can keep continuous mindfulness of this one Buddha, in this mindfulness you can see all the buddhas of the past, present, and future. Why? The merit of mindfulness of one Buddha is infinite and boundless, and one with the merits accomplished by all the infinite numbers of buddhas. The Inconceivable Buddha Dharma is everywhere equal and without distinctions: all buddhas ride upon One Suchness, achieving supreme true enlightenment, equipped with all the countless accomplished virtues and infinite eloquence. All those who enter one-practice *samādhi* like this know that there is no sign of difference in the realm of reality of all the countless buddhas. Whatever they do, their bodies, minds, and inner hearts are forever at the site of enlightenment. All their actions and conduct are *bodhi*."

The *Contemplation of Samantabhadra Sūtra* says: "The sea of all karmic barriers arises from false forms. If you want to repent, sit upright and be mindful of Reality." This is called the supreme repentance. Eliminate the mentality of the three poisons, the mind that clings to objects. If the mind that is aware and contemplating is continuously mindful of Buddha, suddenly there will be clarity and stillness, and there are no more thoughts linked to objects.

The *Great Prajñāpāramitā Sūtra* says: "To have no objects of thought is called mindfulness of buddha." What is meant by "having no objects of thought"? Being mindful of the buddha-mind is called "having no objects of thought." There is no separate Buddha apart from mind, and no other mind apart from Buddha. To be mindful of Buddha is to be mindful of mind. To seek mind is to seek Buddha. Why? Consciousness has no shape, Buddha has no form. Knowing this truth *is* pacifying mind. With constant mindfulness of Buddha, grasping at objects does not arise. Then it is totally formless, everywhere equal and without duality. When you enter this station, the mind that [actively] remembers Buddha fades away and no longer has to be summoned. When you witness this type of mind, this is the true reality-nature body of the Tathāgata. It is also called the Correct Dharma, buddha-nature, the real identity of all phenomena, reality itself. It is also called the Pure Land. It is also called *bodhi*, diamond *samādhi*, fundamental enlightenment, and so on. It is also called the realm of *nirvāṇa*, and *prajñā*, and the like. Though the names are countless, they all share one and the same essence. There is no sense of the subject observing and the object observed.

This level of mind must be made pure and clean, so it is always appearing before you, and no entangling objects can interfere with you. Why [can't they interfere]? Because [for this level of mind] all things and events are the single reality body of the Tathāgata. Abiding in this state of mind, all interlinked vexations will be eliminated of themselves. In an atom of dust are contained infinite worlds; infinite worlds can be gathered into a single pore. Because at root all phenomena are Thus, they do not interfere with each other. The *Huayan Sūtra* says: "Within an atom of dust appear all the phenomena of all the worlds in the cosmos."

[Daoxin taught:] Let us outline pacifying mind: it cannot be expounded in full. The proper skill at it comes from one's own innermost heart. To be brief, for the sake of the doubts of people in the future, let us pose a question: "If the Tathāgata's body of reality is like this, then why does he also have the body of the marks of excellence appearing in the world and preaching the Dharma?"

Daoxin said: It is precisely because the Tathāgata's reality-nature body is pure and perfect that all kinds of forms appear within it. Yet the reality-nature body gives rise to them mindlessly. It is like a glass mirror hung up in a high hall: all images appear within it, but the mirror is mindless, though it can manifest all kinds [of images]. The *Nirvāṇa Sūtra* says: "The Tathāgata appears in the world and preaches the Dharma because of the false thinking of sentient beings." If practitioners cultivate mind until it is totally purified, they realize that "the Tathāgata never preached the Dharma." Only this is complete learning—learning that is formless and [embraces] all forms.

Therefore the *sūtra* says: "Since there are numberless [types of] capacities among sentient beings, [the buddhas] preach the Dharma in numberless ways. Since the Dharma is preached in numberless ways, the meanings are also numberless. Numberless meanings are born from the One Reality. The One Reality is formless, but there is no form that it does not give form to: it is called the true form. This is total purity."

These trustworthy words are our witness. When sitting we must be aware of the onward flow of the conscious mind from its first movement. We must make ourselves aware of its comings and goings and test it with diamond wisdom. For example, plants have no separate knowledge. Knowledge without objects of knowledge is called all-knowledge. This is the One-Form Dharma Gate of bodhisattvas.

Question: What is a Chan master, a meditation teacher?

Daoxin said: Someone who is not disturbed by stillness or confusion, that is, someone who is good at Chan use of mind. If one always abides in cessation, the mind sinks into oblivion. If one always abides in contemplation, the mind scatters in confusion. The *Lotus Sūtra* says: "The Buddha himself abides in the Great Vehicle: the Dharma he attains is adorned with the power of concentration and wisdom, and he uses these to deliver sentient beings."

Question: How can we understand the characteristics of the Dharma? How can we illuminate and purify our minds?

Daoxin said: Not by reciting the buddha-name, not by restricting mind, not by observing mind, not by calculating thought, not by contemplation, not by the practice of observation, not by scattering and confusion. Just let it roll along: don't make it go, don't let it stay. In the solitary purity, the ultimate locus, mind of itself is illuminated and pure. If we can observe it truly, mind is instantly illuminated and pure, mind is like a clear mirror. If we can observe it truly for a year, it will be even more clear and pure; if for three years or five years, even more clear and pure. Some can find understanding by hearing people explain for them. Some never need explanations to understand. A *sūtra* says: "The real identity of the mind of sentient beings is like a precious pearl submerged in water. When the water is turbid, the pearl is hidden. When the water is clear, the pearl is revealed."

Because they slander the Three Jewels and disrupt the harmony of the Samgha, because they are polluted with opinions and vexations, because they are stained by craving and anger and ignorance, sentient beings do not awaken to the fundamental eternal purity of the real identity of mind. Thus, when they study, they grasp understanding in different degrees. These differences generally come from their differences in capacities and causal conditions. To be a teacher for people, one must be good at recognizing these differences.

The *Huayan Sūtra* says: "The form of Samantabhadra's body is like empty space. It is based on Thusness, not on a buddha-land." When you understand, buddhalands are also all Thus, so the land of Thusness depends on nothing at all.

The *Nirvāṇa Sūtra* says: "There is a bodhisattva with a boundless body equal in extent to empty space." It also says: "Because he has the light of goodness, he is like the summer sun." It also says: "Because his body is boundless, it is called Great Nirvāṇa. It also says: "Great Nirvāṇa—its nature is vast."

There are four kinds of people who study. The highest are those with practice, with understanding, and with realization. Next are those with understanding and realization but without practice. Next are those with practice and understanding but without realization. Lowest are those with practice, but without understanding or realization.

Question: In the moment, how should we practice contemplation?

Daoxin said: You must let it roll.

Question: Should we orient ourselves toward the Western Paradise or not?

Daoxin said: If you know that mind is fundamentally unborn and undestroyed and ultimately pure, this *is* the pure buddha-land. There is no further need to face toward the west. The *Huayan Sūtra* speaks of infinite aeons in a moment of thought, and a moment of thought lasting infinite aeons. We must realize that in one direction there are countless directions, and that countless directions are but one direction. For the sake of beings of dull capacities, Buddha had them orient themselves to the Western Paradise: this was not propounded for people of sharp faculties.

Bodhisattvas of profound practice enter birth and death to transform and deliver living beings, without any of the views of sentimental love. If you see sentient beings as having birth and death, yourself as the subject able to save them, and the sentient beings as the objects being saved, then you are not to be called a bodhisattva. Delivering sentient beings is like delivering emptiness —has there ever been any coming or going? The *Diamond Sūtra* says: "In the final deliverance of numberless beings, in reality there are no beings gaining final deliverance."

The first-stage bodhisattva first witnesses everything as empty, then witnesses everything as not empty. This is nondiscriminating wisdom. And this is form: form *is* emptiness. It is not emptiness that wipes out form: form by nature is empty. Bodhisattvas cultivate and learn emptiness as their realization. When new students directly see emptiness, this is seeing emptiness; it is not real emptiness. Those who cultivate the Path until they find real emptiness do not view things as empty or not empty —they have no views. You must understand properly the meaning of form and emptiness.

To learn the use of mind, you must have the mind-road illuminated and pure, and you must understand the characteristics of phenomena completely and clearly. Only then are you fit to be a teacher to people. Moreover, this requires inner and outer to correspond, and theory and practice not to contradict each other. You must break with written and spoken words, and with contrived versions of the Sagely Path. In unity and purity you experience for yourself the fruits of the Path.

There are people who teach living beings for the sake of fame and profit, without comprehending the characteristics of the ultimate Dharma. They do not recognize relative degrees of depth and shallowness in [their pupils'] capacities and causal affinities. They give their seal of approval to everyone, to people who seem enlightened but are otherwise. This is most painful! It is a great disaster! Whenever someone seems illuminated and pure in their perception of mind, they immediately give their approval. These people are gravely damaging the teaching of enlightenment: they are deceiving themselves and deceiving others. People who use mind with such divergences [from the Correct Path] and present this appearance have not found Mind. Those who truly find Mind recognize it clearly for themselves. After a long while the Dharma Eye opens by itself and is well able to distinguish what is empty and false.

Some people reckon that the body is [ultimately] empty and nonexistent, and that the real identity of mind is also obliterated. These are people with nihilistic views. They are the same as outsiders—they are not Buddhists.

Some people reckon that mind is existent and not destroyed. These are people with eternalist views. They, too, are the same as outsiders.

The Buddhists of today who understand clearly do not think that the real identity of mind is obliterated. They are always saving sentient beings, but without creating any sentimental perceptions. They always study wisdom, so that wisdom and folly are everywhere equal. They are always in Chan concentration, so that stillness and confusion are not two. They always view sentient beings as not existent, as ultimately neither born nor destroyed. They manifest forms everywhere, but they have no views or perceptions. They completely understand everything without grasping or rejecting. Without their dividing their bodies, their bodies appear everywhere throughout the worlds of the realm of reality.

Again: In the olden days Chan Master Zhiyi [of Tiantai] taught: "The method of studying the Path requires that understanding and practice support each other. First, find out the source of mind, its essential body and its functions. See inner truth clearly: comprehend completely and distinctly without confusion. After that, the work can be completed."

Understand one, and a thousand follow. Be deluded about one, and you are confused about ten thousand. Lose it by a hair's-breadth, and go wrong by a thousand miles. These are not empty words!

The *Amitabha Sūtra* says: "The *dharmakāya* of all the buddhas enters the minds and thoughts of all sentient beings."

Is it that mind is buddha, or that mind makes buddha? We must realize that mind *is* buddha—outside of mind there is no other buddha. In brief, there are five types [of approaches to this truth].

One: by realizing that the mind-essence is by nature pure and clean, that this essence is the same as buddha.

Two: By realizing that the mind-function produces Dharma jewels and creates eternal quiescence, that the myriad forms of delusion are all Thus.

Three: By always awakening without stopping, so that the awakened mind is always present, aware that Reality is formless.

Four: By constantly contemplating bodily existence as empty and still, inner and outer pervaded and equalized, entering bodily into the realm of reality without obstruction.

Fifth: By preserving unity and not stirring, always abiding through motion and stillness, enabling the learner to clearly see buddha-nature and quickly enter the gate of concentration.

The various scriptures are replete with many methods of contemplation. In what the Great Teacher [Daoxin] expounded, he just made "preserving unity and not stirring" his topic.

[Daoxin taught:] First you must cultivate the contemplation of bodily existence, taking the body as the basis. This bodily existence is composed of the four great elements and the five *skandha*s: in the end it reverts to impermanence and cannot get free. Even while not yet destroyed, it is ultimately empty. The *Vimalakīrti Sūtra* says: "This body is like floating clouds that change and pass away in a moment."

Again: Always contemplate your own bodily existence as being empty and pure as a reflection—it is visible, but it cannot be grasped. Knowledge is born from among the reflections, ultimately without location. Without moving, it responds to beings, in transformations without

[57]

end. In the void are born the six sense faculties: the six sense faculties, too, are empty and still. You must understand completely that the six sense objects that are put opposite them are dreamlike illusions.

When the eye sees things, the things are not there in the eye. It is like a mirror reflecting the image of a face with complete clarity. In the void appear shapes and images. In the mirror there is not a thing: evidently the person's face is not in the mirror, and the mirror does not go out into the person's face. Investigating in detail like this, we realize that from the beginning neither the mirror nor the face has ever gone out or gone in, gone or come. This is the meaning of *tathāgata,* "the one who has come from Thusness."

By this close analysis [we find that] in the eye and in the mirror from the beginning it has always been empty and still. The mirror's reflecting and the eye's reflecting are the same. Taking this as the point of comparison, [we find that] all the sense faculties are this way as well. We know that the eye is fundamentally empty, so whatever form is seen we must know is alien form. When the ears hear sound, we know it is alien sound. When the nose smells scents, we know they are alien scents. When the tongue differentiates flavors, we know they are alien flavors. When the conceptual mind stands opposite phenomena, we know they are alien phenomena. When the body receives touch, we know it is alien touch. To contemplate like this and reach such knowledge is contemplating empty stillness.

When you see form with such knowledge, you do not receive form. Not receiving form is emptiness, emptiness is formless, formlessness is uncontrived. This is the gate of liberation. For the learner who finds liberation, all the senses are like this: no need to repeat the account for each one.

Be constantly mindful that the six sense faculties are empty and still, and that you have no hearing or seeing. The *Bequeathed Teaching Sutra* says: "This time is the middle of the night, still and soundless." You must know that the Dharma preached by the Tathāgata takes empty stillness as the basis. Be ever mindful that the six senses are empty and still; be constantly as if in the middle of the night. What is seen and heard by day are all things external to the body. Let it be always empty and pure within the body, preserving unity without stirring. With this eye of emptiness and purity, focus the attention and observe one thing. No matter whether it is day or night, focus the energy so that it does not move. When the mind is about to run off and scatter, quickly gather it back. It is like tying a bird's foot so that when it wishes to fly away, it is held fast. Contemplate without stopping all the time: when purified, mind will stabilize itself. The *Vimalakīrti Sūtra* says: "Gathering in mind is the site of enlightenment." This is a method for gathering in mind. The *Lotus Sūtra* says: "Having eliminated sleep and gathered in mind for countless ages, by the accomplished merit of this he was able to engender meditative concentrations." This was said also in the *Bequeathed Teaching Sūtra:* "Mind is the ruler of the five faculties: control it in one place, and all will be accomplished."

The foregoing are true principles of the Great Vehicle. All are laid out on the basis of scripture: they are not false words outside the truth. These [forms of practice described above] are stainless activities, and ultimate meanings. They go beyond the stage of the *śrāvaka*s and go straight for the bodhisattva Path.

Those who hear should practice: don't be doubtful and confused. It is like a person learning archery. At first he shoots at large targets. By and by he can hit smaller and smaller ones. Then he can hit a single feather, then hit it and smash it into a hundred pieces, then hit one of the hundredths. Then he can shoot the arrow before with the arrow after, and hit the notch, so the arrows line up one after another and he does not let any arrows fall.

This is a metaphor for practicing the Path, concentrating the mind from thought-instant to thought-instant, going on continuously from mind-moment to mind-moment without any interruptions, so that correct mindfulness is not broken and appears before you. Another *sūtra* says: "With the arrow of wisdom, shoot through the gate of triple liberation. Let the arrows line up and hold each other up so that none fall."

Again: [Studying the Path] is like drilling for fire. If you stop before it gets hot, though you may wish to get fire, it is impossible.

[Studying the Path is] also like this: A family had a wish-fulfilling gem. Whatever they sought they got. Unexpectedly they lost it, but they remember it and never forget it.

Again: It is like a poison arrow entering the flesh. The shaft has been pulled out, but the point is still in there. Suffering pain like this, there is no forgetting it even temporarily: it is constantly in mind. [A person studying the Path] must be like this.

The secret essence of this Dharma cannot be transmitted to the wrong person. It is not that we are reluctant to pass it on: it is that we fear that people will not believe and will fall into the crime of slandering the Dharma. We must choose the right people: we cannot be in a hurry or speak hastily. Take care! Take care! Though the Dharma sea is immeasurable, it is traveled in a single word. When you find the meaning you forget the word. Not using even a single word, yet knowing with complete comprehension like this—this is getting the Buddha's meaning.

When beginning students sit in meditation, in undivided stillness they directly contemplate body and mind. They must investigate the four elements and the five *skandhas*, eyes, ears, nose, tongue, body feeling, and conceptual mind, greed, anger, and ignorance, along with all phenomena, whether good or bad, hostile or friendly, ordinary or holy. They must observe that all these are originally empty and still, unborn and undestroyed, everywhere equal and without duality. Since the beginning there has been nothing at all, just ultimate quiescent extinction. Since the beginning, just pure liberation. You must do this contemplation always, no matter whether day or night, whether you are walking, standing, sitting, or lying down.

If you do, you will realize that your own bodily existence is like the moon in the water, like an image in a mirror, like a mirage when it is hot, like an echo in an empty valley. If you say it exists, wherever you seek it, it cannot be seen. If you say it does not exist, when you comprehend completely, it is always before your eyes. The buddhas' body of reality is also like this. Then you come to know that from countless ages past your own body has ultimately never been born, and that in the future ultimately there is no one who dies. If you can always do this contemplation, this is true repentance: the heavy evil *karma* of thousands of ages dissipates of itself.

Only those who are confused by doubts and who cannot engender faith are incapable of enlightenment. If you believe and practice according to this [contemplation method], all of you will get to enter into the unborn truth.

Again: When you become aware of mind arising linked to other objects, immediately contemplate this arising and view it as ultimately not arising. See that when this mental attachment arises, it does not come from anywhere or go to anywhere. As you constantly contemplate the process of grasping at objects, you observe the thoughts and mixed mindfulness of false consciousness. When the mind of confusion does not arise, you attain the coarse level of abiding. When you find the mind that abides, there are no more thoughts linked to objects, and everything is accordingly still and steady. You also attain the appropriate cessation of afflictions: you have finished with the old ones and do not create any new ones. This is called contemplation that liberates.

[With this contemplation], even if the mind creates afflictions and becomes depressed, confused, and sunk in dark torpor, it soon disperses this and adjusts itself.

Mind is slowly put at peace and made to find its proper state. When mind of itself is peaceful and clean, then all that is needed is bold advance, as if saving your head from burning. You must not slack off or get lazy. Try hard, try hard!

When beginners sit in meditation to contemplate mind: Sit alone someplace. First straighten out your body and sit upright; let your robe be wide and your belt loose. Let your body relax: rub yourself down seven or eight times. Let the exhalations from the belly through the throat cease. Then you will find in abundance the purity, emptiness, and peace of inherent reality-nature.

When body and mind are properly attuned, when mind and spirit are at peace, then in deep mystic fusion, the breath is pure and cool. Slowly gather in mind until the path of the spirit is pure and sharp and the mind-ground is illumined and pure. As you perceive clearly and distinctly, inner and outer are empty and pure—this is the mind's inherent *nirvāṇa*. With this *nirvāṇa*, the mind of the sages is manifest. Though its real nature is formless, intent and proportion always remain. Thus, the profound luminous one never ends: it remains forever shining bright. This is called the buddha-nature, the enlightened real identity. Those who see buddha-nature leave behind forever birth and death: they are called people who transcend the world.

Therefore the *Vimalakīrti Sūtra* says: "Emptying through, one returns to find original mind." How trustworthy these words are! One who awakenes to buddha-nature is called a bodhisattva, a person who has awakened to the Path, a person who has arrived, a person who has found reality-nature. Thus the *sūtra* says: "A phrase that has profound spiritual energy lasts through the ages without decaying."

The expedient means explained above are for beginners. We know that there are expedient means for cultivating the Path: this is where the intentions of the sages meet.

In general, methods of relinquishing personal existence begin with stabilizing and emptying mind, and make mind and objects quiescent and still. These methods recast thinking into mystic quiescence, so that mind does not stir and the reality-nature of mind is still and settled. Then you cut off grasping at objects. Deeply fused, solidified in purity, mind is empty, everywhere equal, peaceful, and still. Material forces are totally gone: you abide in the pure body of reality, no longer subject to states of being.

If you stir up mind and lose mindfulness, you will not avoid being subject to birth. Things must be like this: this is the mental state predetermined [by losing mindfulness]. This is a contrived phenomenon. Reality is fundamentally without [such contrived] phenomena. Only reality without such phenomena is called reality. Thus, reality is uncontrived: uncontrived reality is true reality. Thus the *sūtra* says: "Empty, without contrivance, without wishes, without form—this is true liberation." In this sense, true reality is uncontrived. The methods of relinquishing personal existence employ constant contemplation of the body: illuminating the ground of mind and mental objects, you use this spiritual illumination to dispense with [personal existence].

The Great Teacher [Daoxin] said: Zhuang Zi speaks of the oneness of heaven and earth, and the oneness of the myriad things therein. A *sūtra* says: "The one is not one. [Oneness is propounded] to refute the multiplicity of objects. When this is heard of by people with shallow consciousness, they think that the one is one." Thus, Zhuang Zi is still stuck on oneness. Lao Zi says: "How profound! How deep! Within it there is a vital energy." Externally, [this formulation] is formless, but inside it still keeps mind. The *Huayan Sūtra* says: "You do not become attached to dualistic things, because there is neither one nor two." The *Vimalakīrti Sūtra* says: "Mind is neither inside nor outside nor in between." By such testimony we know that Lao Zi is stuck on the vital energy's consciousness. The *Nirvāṇa Sūtra* says: "All sentient beings have buddha-nature. How can it be said that inanimate things are without buddha-nature? [If so], how could they expound the Dharma?" Vasubandhu's [*Consciousness Only*] treatise says: "[Buddha's] response bodies and transformation bodies are not the real Buddha, not the ones that expound the Dharma."

SECTION SIX

Great Teacher Hongren of Youju Temple on Shuangfeng Mountain in Jizhou
Tang Period

The one who took it up after Chan Master Daoxin was Hongren. Hongren transmitted the Dharma and was an honored man of the Subtle Wondrous Dharma. In his time [his school] was called the Pure Gate of East Mountain. Because monks and laymen in the metropolitan region acclaimed East Mountain in Jizhou for having a lot of people who found the fruit [of enlightenment], it was called the East Mountain Dharma Gate.

Someone asked: "To study the Path, why do you not go to cities and towns but instead live in the mountains?"

[Hongren] answered: "The timbers for a great hall come from the remote valleys, not from inhabited areas. Because they are far from humans, they have not been chopped down or damaged by their axes. One by one they grow into giant things: only then are they fit to serve as the ridgebeams.

"Thus we know how to rest the spirit in remote valleys, to stay far away from the hubbub and dust, to nourish our true nature in the mountains and forswear conventional affairs always. When there is nothing before the eyes, mind of itself is peaceful. From this the

tree of the Path blooms and the fruits of the Chan forest
come forth."

The Great Teacher Hongren sat alone in purity.. He
produced no written record. He explained mystic truth
orally and imparted it to people in silence. There is a
book in circulation on Chan technique said to be by Chan
Master Hongren, but this is spurious.

According to *Record of the People and the Teaching of
the Laṅkāvatāra* (*Leng jia ren fa zhi*), compiled by the
monk Xuanze of Shoushan in Anzhou:

Hongren's lay surname was Zhou. His ancestors were
people of Xunyang, registered in Huangmeixian. His
father early on abandoned them, and he was burdened by
the filial duty to support his mother.

He started to serve Chan Master Daoxin at the age of
seven. After leaving home he dwelt at Youju Temple.
He occupied himself with delivering beings with ever-
increasing compassion: the intent within him was noble
and pure. He kept his mouth shut in the arena of affir-
mation and denial. In environments of form and void,
his mind was fused. People worked to support him, and
Dharma companions sat at his feet as disciples. Balancing
his mind, he took as his task contemplation of the cosmos:
the Teacher was indeed illuminated in his contemplative
perception. [For Hongren,] walking, standing, sitting
and lying down were all sites of enlightenment; actions
of body, mouth, and mind were all the business of the
buddhas. For him there was no duality between stillness
and confusion, so speech and silence were ever one. During his time people came from all quarters and all classes
to ask for instruction and make him their teacher; they

came to him empty and returned full. Thousands came
month after month. During his lifetime he bequeathed
no written works, but his truth was in accord with the
mystic message.

During that period Chan Master Shenxiu of Jingzhou
submitted to his lofty standards and personally received
Hongren's charge. Xuanze came to Shuangfeng in 670
and respectfully received Hongren's teachings: he served
him for five years in all, going there and back three
times.

Monks and nuns and laypeople alike gathered around
Hongren, working to provide support. He taught them
the meaning of the *Laṅkāvatāra Sūtra*, saying: "Only
those who witness it with their minds fully know this
scripture—it is not something that verbal analyses can
explain."

In the second month of 674, Hongren ordered
Xuanze and the others to erect a stupa. All the disciples
joined to transport naturally square stones, until they had
built a very imposing and beautiful structure. On the
fourteenth day of the month, Hongren asked if the stupa
had been completed. Told that it had been, Hongren
said: "If we cannot share the day of the Buddha's *nirvāṇa*,
then we have been considering as a Buddhist monastery
what really has been a secular dwelling."

He also said: "In my life I have taught numberless
people. Many good ones have perished. I only give approval to ten as the ones who can transmit my path in the
future. With Shenxiu I have discussed the *Laṅkāvatāra
Sūtra*, and he has penetrated its mystic truth: he is sure
to bring much benefit. Zhixian of Zizhou and Registrar

Liu of White Pine Mountain both have refined natures. Huizang of Xinzhou and Xuanyue of Suizhou I recall [as worthy, though now] I don't see them. Old An of Songshan profoundly practices the Path. Faru of Luzhou, Huineng of Shaozhou, and the Korean monk Zhide of Yangzhou are all fit to be people's teachers, but will only be local figures. Yifang of Yuezhou will continue to lecture and preach." To Xuanze he said: "You yourself must properly maintain and cherish your combined practice. After I die you and Shenxiu must make the sun of enlightenment radiate anew and the lamp of mind shine again."

On the sixteenth day of the month, Hongren asked [the assembly]: "Do you know my mind now or not?" Xuanze took it upon himself to answer: "We do not know." The Great Teacher Hongren then indicated the ten directions with his hand: "Each and every one sets out the mind that is realized." At midday on the sixteenth, Hongren faced south and sat quietly: he closed his eyes and died. He was seventy-four years old.

He was entombed in a stupa on Fengmao Mountain. Even today [his body] looks the way it ordinarily did in the past. There is a wall portrait of him at Anzhou Temple by Lu Zichan of Fanyang. Li Huixiu of Longxi, formerly Minister of the Department of War, composed a eulogy:

"What a marvel was the Master! In mystic accord with the reality of the Path, he gathered in his mind and cut off intellectual knowledge. With lofty enlightenment, he penetrated the spirit: free of birth, he realized the fruit: showing extinction, he shared the dusts. Here and now he has been transformed: how soon will anyone approach his level?"

The Great Teacher Hongren said: "There is a room —it is filled with filth and debris. What is it?" He also said: "When all the filth and debris have been totally swept away, there is nothing at all. What is it?"

[Hongren also taught:] When you are sitting, settle your face, arrange your body properly, and sit straight. Relax your body and mind. Through all of space, see as from afar a single word. There is an inherent sequence. People of beginner's mentality do a lot of grasping at objects. You should contemplate a single word in your mind for now. After you experience realization, as you are sitting, it will look like this: In the midst of a vast wilderness, far off, standing all alone, is a high mountain. You are sitting on open ground on top of the mountain, looking off into the distance in all directions. There are no boundaries. As you sit, you fill the world. Relaxing and releasing body and mind, you abide in the buddha-realm. The pure body of reality, which is limitless, can also be described like this.

Hongren also said: "Just when you witness the great body of reality, who is witnessing it?"

He also said: "There are thirty-two marks of the Buddha. Does the jar also have them? Does the pillar? Do earth and wood and tile and stone also have the thirty-two marks or not?"

Another time, he took up a couple of firebrands. Holding a long one and a short one together, he asked: "Which one is long? Which one is short?"

He also said: "There appears someone lighting a lamp

and creating the myriad things. Everyone says that this someone is creating dreams and working magic. Some say he doesn't create or make—everything is all great final *nirvāṇa.*"

He also said: "Completely comprehending birth is the Dharma of birthlessness. It is not that there is birthlessness apart from the phenomena of birth. Nāgārjuna said: 'Phenomena are neither born of themselves nor born of others nor born of [self and others] together, nor are they born without a causal basis. Thus we know: there is no birth.' Since phenomena are born of causes, they have no inherent identity of their own. Since they have no self-nature, how can phenomena exist [in an absolute sense]?"

He also said: "Empty space has no center. The bodies of the buddhas are also like this. This is where I will give you the seal of approval for complete perception of buddha-nature."

He also said: "Right when you are in the temple sitting in meditation, is your body there under the trees in the forest sitting in meditation too, or not? Can all the [inanimate things such as] earth, wood, tiles, and stone also sit in meditation or not? Can earth, wood, tiles, and stone see form, hear sound, put on a robe, carry a bowl? The *Laṅkāvatāra Sūtra* speaks of the '*dharmakāya* of objects' —it is this."

Shenxiu, the Great Teacher of Yuquan Temple in Jingzhou Xuanze, the Great Teacher of Shoushan Temple in Anzhou An, the Great Teacher of Huishan Temple on Mount Song in Luozhou

These three Great Teachers were national teachers during the reign of Heavenly Great Sage Empress, the Spirit Dragon Responding to Heaven, Her Supreme Majesty (Ze Tian, r. 684–704). They all succeeded to Chan Master Hongren, who gave them predictions of enlightenment (and included them among the sanctioned ones) when he said: "I only give approval to ten as the ones who can transmit my path in the future."

The *Record of the People and the Teaching of the Lankāvatāra*, compiled by Xuanze of Shoushan in Anzhou, says:

Chan Master Shenxiu: His lay surname was Li, and he was from Weishi in Bianzhou. He took long journeys, intent on the Path. He came to Chan Master Hongren's place on Shuangfeng Mountain in Jizhou, and received the Chan teaching. [In Shenxiu] the Chan lamp shone silently, the verbal route was cut off; his mental machinations were wiped out, and he pro-

duced no written records. Later he dwelled at Yuquan
Temple in Jingzhou. In 701 he was summoned to the
Eastern Capital. Following the court, he traveled back
and forth between the two capitals, teaching, and served
in person as the Imperial Teacher.

Zetian, the Great Sage Empress, asked Chan Master
Shenxiu: "The Dharma you transmit is the message of
whose house?" Shenxiu answered: "I have received the
Dharma of East Mountain in Jizhou." The Empress
asked: "What text do you base yourself on?" Shenxiu
answered: "We go by the one-practice *samādhi* of the
Prajñā Sūtra Spoken by Mañjuśrī." The Empress said:
"For cultivating the Path, none goes beyond the Dharma
Gate of East Mountain." Since Shenxiu was a disciple of
Hongren [on East Mountain], this became his sanction
[from the empress].

On the thirteenth day of the third month of 705, an
imperial decree was issued [praising Shenxiu thus]:

"The Chan Master's tracks are far from the dusts of
the conventional world. His spirit roams beyond the
material world. He is in accord with the subtle truth of
formlessness, and he transforms the deluded paths of
those in bondage. [In him,] the water of concentration is clear inwardly and the pearl of discipline is
all-pervasive outwardly. Disciples turn their minds to
Buddhism and travel across the country, hoping for instruction at his Dharma Gate, longing to meet a Leader
on the Path."

In his later years Chan Master Shenxiu wanted to
return to his home area, but this was not permitted. Since
his intent was so lofty, he was not stuck in longings for

home. The writings he left behind show his ideas: he
pointed things out without a lot of talk. The Chan Master
faithfully served two emperors and taught at the two
capitals: both court and countryside benefited. He delivered innumerable people. By imperial decree a Bao En
Temple was set up in his hometown.

On the twenty-eighth day of the second month of 706
at Heavenly Palace Temple in the Eastern Capital, as he
sat quietly without illness, he imparted three words of
instruction: "*Bend* the *crooked* and make it *straight*," and
died. He was more than a hundred years old. He had
brought together the monks and nuns and laymen and
laywomen of the city and caused Buddhist establishments
to be embellished on a wide scale. He was ceremonially
entombed on Longmen Mountain. The grandees and
lords all offered epitaphs. There was an imperial decree:

The late Chan Master Shenxiu—subtle consciousness
outwardly fused, workings of spiritual awareness inwardly penetrated, he has probed the inner recesses of
nonduality. Indeed he has found the topknot jewel: he
guards the gate of true oneness. Hanging up the mind-
mirror alone, he perfects luminous awareness and responds to beings. He joins with form with his spirit
illumined, without contrived activity, staying independent: sense objects are purified and entanglements are
banished. For a hundred years he grew more and more
intent: day by day his energy became more refined. Only
then could he see through to the mystic subtlety of the
consciousness that is before us and be a guide to the eyes
and ears of many beings. Without employing conceptual
consciousness, with great compassion he shared the exis-

tence [of all beings], teaching them carefully, following timely expedients. Once people run afoul of "plaster sun" theories [that cling to contrived models of reality], they are always thinking of teachings transmitted by conceptual consciousness. Though [Shenxiu found] that inner truth is nameless and formless, and he was not dependent on people offering veneration, nevertheless, he was very scrupulous with the teacher–pupil relationship, and he wished to glorify [Buddhism]. He should be given the title "Chan Master of Great Pervasiveness."

Another imperial edict ordered the dispatch of Lu Zhengquan, Lead Rider to the Heir Apparent, to escort [Shenxiu's corpse] to Jingzhou back to his disciples. An official plaque for their monastery was also entrusted to Lu Zhengquan, who was to go there and report back. Shenxiu's disciples said: "How perfect our Teacher was! He had traveled the Path to the end and reached the real truth, pure liberation, perfectly illuminated reality. He expounded the Supreme Path and opened the way to Supreme Wisdom. His tracks were obliterated in the One Mind, oblivious of past, present, and future. He temporarily used words to reveal the inner truth and followed the inner truth to reach accord. He acted always as a Dharma ferry, taking people across without making them objects of salvation.

The Great Teacher Shenxiu said: "The *Nirvāṇa Sūtra* says: 'If you properly understand a single word, you are called a Vinaya Master.' The text comes from the *sūtra:* the proof lies within you."

He also said: "Does this mind have mind or not? What mind is this mind?

[75]

He also said: "When you see form, is the form there or not? What form is this form?"

He also said: "When you hear the sound of a bell being struck, is the sound there when the bell is struck or before the bell is struck? What sound is this sound?"

He also said: "Is the sound of the bell being struck only there within the temple? Is the sound of the bell also there throughout the worlds of the ten directions?"

He also said: "The body perishes but its shadow does not. The bridge is flowing, not the river."

He also said: "The teaching of my Path is subsumed under the two words *essence* and *function*. It is also called 'the double mystic gate.' It is also called 'turning the Dharma wheel.' It is also called 'the fruit of the Path.'"

He also said: "See before seeing. When seeing, see and see again."

He also said: "The *Bodhisattva Necklace Sūtra* says: 'Bodhisattvas perceive and are still. Buddhas are still and perceive.'"

He also said: "A mustard seed goes into Mount Sumeru; Mount Sumeru goes into a mustard seed."

Seeing a bird fly by, he asked: "What is it?"

He also said: "Can you sit in meditation on the tips of the tree branches and banish time?"

He also said: "Can you pass straight through a wall or not?"

He also said: "The *Nirvāṇa Sūtra* says there is a bodhisattva with a boundless body who comes from the east. Since the bodhisattva's body is boundless, when then does he come from the east? Why not from the west, the south, or the north?

SECTION EIGHT

Chan Master Puji of Song Gao Mountain in Luozhou
Chan Master Jingxian of Mount Song
Chan Master Yifu of Orchid Mountain, Changan
Chan Master Huifu of Jade Mountain in Lantian

Puji, Jingxian, Yifu, and Huifu all learned the necessary practices for Dharma companions from the Teacher Shenxiu, and all succeeded to him. All of them had left home while young and practiced pure discipline. They had sought out teachers to ask about the Path, making long journeys to visit Chan centers. They came to Yuquan Temple in Jingzhou and met Shenxiu, receiving from him the Chan Dharma. All these masters served the Great Teacher Shenxiu more than ten years, until they emptied out and witnessed for themselves the pearl of Chan shining alone.

The Great Teacher charged Puji, Jingxian, Yifu, and Huifu to be great lamps illuminating the world, to transmit the great mirror. People doing sitting meditation throughout the country acclaimed these four Chan Masters, saying: "The Dharma mountain is pure, the Dharma sea is clear, the Dharma mirror is bright, the

Dharma lamp is illuminated." They sat quietly on famous mountains and clarified their spirits in hidden valleys. Their virtues merged with the ocean of reality-nature, their practices flourished in an abundance of the branches of Chan. Pure and clean, without contrived action, they walked alone in silent serenity. The Lamp of Chan shines in silence: those who learn all witness the buddha-mind.

Since the Song period (420–477) there have been Chan Teachers of great virtue to take it up generation after generation. Starting from Gunabhadra in the [Liu-] Song dynasty, the Lamp has been passed through the generations until the Tang dynasty, eight generations in all. These comprised twenty-four men who attained the Path and harvested the Fruit.

Bodhidharma's Treatise on Contemplating Mind

HUIKE ASKED: If there are people intent on seeking the Path of Enlightenment, what method should they practice, what method is most essential and concise?

Bodhidharma answered: Let them just contemplate mind—this one method takes in all practices, and is indeed essential and concise.

Huike asked: How can one method take in all practices?

Bodhidharma answered: Mind is the root of the myriad phenomena. All phenomena are born from mind. If you can completely comprehend mind, the myriad practices are complete. It is like a great tree: all the branches and flowers and fruits grow based on the root. The tree grows only if the root survives. If the root is cut, the tree is sure to die. If you cultivate the Path by comprehending mind, you save effort and success is easy. If you cultivate the Path without comprehending mind, then you waste effort and there is no benefit. Thus we know that all good and evil come from one's own mind. If you seek outside of mind, it is impossible.

Huike asked: Why is contemplating mind called complete comprehension?

Bodhidharma answered: When the great bodhisattvas practice profound perfection of transcendental wisdom, they comprehend that the four great elements and the five clusters are fundamentally empty and selfless. They see that there are two different kinds of activity initiated by inherent mind: pure states of mind and defiled states of mind. Pure mind is the mind of undefiled True Thusness. Defiled mind is the mind of defilement and ignorance. These two kinds of mind are both there of themselves from the beginning. Though everything is produced by the combination of temporary causes, pure mind always takes delight in good causes, while defiled mind is constantly thinking of evil deeds.

If True Thusness is aware of itself and, being aware, does not accept defilement, then this is called being a sage. This enables one to leave all suffering far behind and experience the bliss of *nirvāṇa*. If you follow along with defilement and create evil, you are subject to its bondage—this is called being an ordinary person. Then you are submerged in the triple world, subject to all kinds of suffering. Why? Because those defiled states of mind block off the body of True Thusness. The *Ten Stages Sūtra* says: "Within the bodies of sentient beings there is an indestructible enlightened nature. It is like the orb of the sun: its body is bright and round and full and vast without limit. Because it is covered by the black clouds of the five clusters, it is like a lamp placed in a jar so that the light cannot appear." The *Nirvāṇa Sūtra* says: "All sentient beings have buddha-nature. Because it is covered over by ignorance, they are not set free. Buddha-nature is enlightenment. When it is aware of itself and its awareness is completely illuminated apart from what covers it, this is called liberation."

Thus we know that all forms of good have enlightenment as their root: the tree of all merits appears based on the root of enlightenment. The fruit of *nirvāṇa* is formed from this. Contemplating mind like this can indeed be called complete comprehension.

Huike also asked: You have just stated that all the merits of the enlightened nature of True Thusness depend on enlightenment as their root. I wonder, what is the root for all the forms of evil of the mind of ignorance?

Bodhidharma answered: Though the mind of ignorance has eighty-four thousand afflictions, sentiments, desires, and uncountable evils, in essence, they all have the three poisons as their root. The three poisons are greed, anger, and ignorance. The mind of these three poisons of itself inherently includes all forms of evil. It is like a great tree: though there is one root, the branches and leaves it gives life to are numberless. Each of the three poisons as a root gives birth to evil deeds even more prolifically. These three poisons become three poisons from a single fundamental essence. They are sure to manifest the six sense faculties, also called the six thieves. The six thieves are the six consciousnesses: they are called six thieves because they go in and out via the sense fac-

ulties becoming attached to the myriad objects and form-
ing evil deeds, which block off the body of True
Thusness.

All sentient beings are plunged into ignorance and
confusion by these three poisons and six thieves. Body
and mind sink down into birth and death and revolve
through the six planes of existence, receiving all kinds of
suffering and affliction. It is like a river that starts from
a small spring: since the flow from the source is unbroken, it can extend its waves for thousands of miles. If a
person cuts off the root source, then the many streams all
stop.

Those who seek liberation must be able to transform
the three poisons into three forms of pure discipline, and
transform the six thieves into the six *pāramitā*s, thereby
spontaneously leaving behind forever all forms of suffering.

Huike asked: The three poisons and the six thieves are
vast and limitless: how can one avoid their infinite pain
by just contemplating mind?

Bodhidharma answered: The karmic rewards of the
triple world are just products of mind. If you can completely comprehend mind, within the triple world you
escape the triple world.

The triple world corresponds to the three poisons.
Greed corresponds to the realm of desire, anger to the
realm of form, and ignorance to the formless realm.
From these three poisons the mind assembles all the
karmic rewards of evil and forms the six planes of *sam-
sāra*. Thus [the three poisons] are called the triple world.
Since the evil created by the three poisons may vary in

seriousness, the rewards received are not the same, but divide into six planes—hence the name "six planes of existence."

Huike asked: How does it divide into six according to the relative seriousness [of the evil deeds]?

Bodhidharma answered: If sentient beings do not comprehend the correct basis [for enlightenment] and cultivate goodness with the mind of delusion, they do not avoid the triple world and birth in one of the three less grievous planes of existence. This means that if in delusion they cultivate the ten virtues and in falsity they seek happiness, they will not avoid the realm of greed and birth in the plane of the *devas*. If in delusion they uphold the fivefold discipline and falsely create love and hate, they will not avoid the realm of anger and birth in the plane of human beings. If in delusion they cling to contrived belief and wrongly seek blessings, they will not avoid the realm of ignorance and birth in the plane of the *asuras*. These three are called the less grievous planes of existence.

What are the three heavy planes of existence? This means that if they indulge the mind of the three poisons and do nothing but evil deeds, they will fall into the three heavy planes of existence. If their deeds of greed are serious, they fall into the plane of hungry ghosts. If their deeds of anger are serious, they fall into the plane of hells. If their deeds of ignorance are serious, they fall into the plane of the animals. These three heavy planes of existence together with the previous three less grievous planes make up the six planes of existence.

Thus we know that evil deeds are born from one's own

mind. If we can keep mind apart from all evil deeds,
then the sufferings of revolving in the triple world and
the six planes of existence will spontaneously melt away.
If we can put an end to all suffering, this is called liberation.

Huike asked: What about the Buddha's statement:
"Only after countless ages and immeasurable effort and
suffering did I achieve enlightenment"? Why do you
now say that just removing the three poisons is called
liberation?

Bodhidharma answered: In words spoken by the Buddha there is no falsity. "Countless ages" refers to the
mind of the three poisons. This mind contains countless
evil thoughts, and each and every thought is an age.
Poisonous evil thoughts are like the sands of the Ganges,
so they are called countless. Once the reality-nature of
True Thusness is covered over by these three evils, how
can it be called liberation unless we transcend all those
countless evil thoughts? In the present case, being able to
remove the mind of the three poisons, greed, anger, and
ignorance, is called "passing over countless ages." Sentient beings in the last age are stupid and their faculties
are dull: they do not understand the extremely profound
and subtle meaning of the Tathāgata. They do not understand the esoteric sense of "countless ages," so they say
that one may become buddha only after passing through
aeons numerous as the dusts. In the final age this cannot
but cause doubts and misapprehension by people cultivating practice and make them retreat from the Path of
enlightenment.

Huike also asked: *Bodhisattva-mahasattva*s become

buddha by upholding the three combinations of pure discipline and by practicing the six perfections. Now you are directing learners only to contemplate mind. If they do not cultivate the practice of discipline, how will they become buddha?

Bodhidharma answered: The three combinations of pure discipline control the mind of the three poisons. To control [even] one of the poisons achieves immeasurable good. "Combination" means "gathered together." They are called the three combinations of pure discipline because using them we can curb the three poisons so that the three immeasurable goods are all gathered together in the mind.

The six perfections mean purifying the six sense faculties. The foreign word *pāramitā* means in our language "reaching the other shore." This is because when the six sense faculties are pure and clean and not stained with wordly dusts, this is equivalent to escaping from affliction and reaching the other shore. Hence the name "the six *pāramitā*s," "the six perfections."

Huike asked: The three combinations of pure discipline spoken of in the scriptures are vowing to cut off all evils, vowing to cultivate all good things, and vowing to deliver all sentient beings. Now you are only saying to control the mind of the three poisons. Does this not contradict the meaning of the scriptures?

Bodhidharma answered: The scriptures expounded by the Buddha are true words, free from falsehood. When *bodhisattva-mahasattvas* were cultivating the practices of bodhisattvas in the past, they made three vows in order to deal with the three poisons, vowing to uphold the three combinations of pure discipline. They always practice discipline, because to deal with the poison of greed, they vow to cut off all evils. They always practice concentration, because to deal with the poison of anger, they vow to cultivate all good things. They always practice wisdom, because to deal with the poison of ignorance, they vow to deliver all sentient beings. Because they uphold these three kinds of pure *dharmas*—discipline, concentration, and wisdom—they go beyond the evil deeds of the three poisons and achieve the path of the buddhas.

Being able to curb the three poisons means that all forms of evil dissolve, hence it is called cutting off [evil]. Being able to uphold the three combinations of pure discipline means that all forms of good are fully present, hence it is called cultivating [good]. Being able to cut off evil and cultivate good means that the myriad practices are perfected, benefiting both self and others, and saving all sentient beings, hence it is called delivering [beings]. Thus we know that the discipline that is cultivated is not apart from mind. If inherent mind is pure, all sentient beings are pure. Thus the *sūtra* says: "When mind is defiled, sentient beings are defiled. When mind is pure, sentient beings are pure." It is also said: "To purify the buddha-land, first purify your mind. As one's mind is purified, so the buddha-land is purified." If you are able to control the three kinds of poisonous mentality, the three combinations of pure discipline are spontaneously perfected.

Huike also asked: As the scriptures explain them, the six *pāramitās*, also called the six perfections, are giving, discipline, patience, energetic progress, meditative concentration, and wisdom. Now you say that if the six sense faculties are pure, this is called the six perfections. If we understand it this way, what is the meaning of "perfection"?

Bodhidharma said: If you want to cultivate the six perfections, you should always be purifying the six sense faculties. First you must subdue the six thieves. If you can abandon the eye-thief and leave behind objects of form, the mind will be free of stinginess—this is called [the perfection of] giving. If you can control the ear-thief and not let it indulge in the dusts of sounds, this is called upholding discipline. If you can subdue the nose-thief and equalize all smells good and bad so that you are independent and properly adjusted, this is called [the perfection of] patience. If you can curb the tongue-thief so that you do not crave illicit flavors, and extol and expound [the Dharma] tirelessly, this is called [the perfection of] energetic progress. If you can subdue the body-thief so that amid all kinds of contacts and desires you are profoundly clear and unmoving, this is called [the perfection of] meditative concentration. If you can attune the conceptual mind-thief so that you do not submit to ignorance, and constantly cultivate enlightened wisdom and enjoy its merits, this is called [the perfection of] wisdom. *Pāramitā* means "crossing." The six *pāramitā*s are likened to boats that can convey sentient beings to the other shore.

Huike asked: According to the scriptures, when the Tathāgata Śākyamuni was a buddha-to-be, he attained enlightenment only after drinking some milk gruel. That is, because he drank the gruel beforehand, he experienced the fruit of enlightenment. This was not simply liberation through contemplating mind.

Bodhidharma answered: What the scripture says is true—there is no falsity. He had to drink the "milk gruel" before he could become buddha. But the milk gruel the Buddha speaks of is not the impure worldly kind. It is the milk of the Tathāgata's pure *dharma*s, namely, the three combinations of pure discipline and the six perfections. When Buddha became enlightened, it was because of drinking this milk of the pure *dharma*s that he experienced the fruit of enlightenment. It would be nothing but slander to say that the Tathāgata partook of the impure, bad-smelling milk mixed of worldly lust and desire. The Tathāgata himself is the indestructible, stainless diamond body of reality, forever detached from worldly sufferings. What need would he have for such impure milk to quench his thirst? As the scripture says: "The cow [that gives the milk of the pure *dharma*s] is not on the high plains and not in the low marshlands. It does not eat grain or chaff. It is not in the same herd with the bulls. The body of this cow is lustrous with purple and gold."

"This cow" refers to Vairocana Buddha. Since his great compassion has sympathy for everyone, from the body of pure *dharma*s he causes to pour forth the subtle wondrous *dharma*-milk of the three disciplines and six perfections. The milk nourishes all those who seek liberation. Not only does the Tathāgata drink this pure milk from a pure cow to attain enlightenment; all sentient beings will achieve ultimate perfect enlightenment if they are able to drink it.

Huike asked: In the scriptures spoken by Buddha, he commands sentient beings to build monasteries, to cast images, to burn incense and scatter flowers, and to keep ever-bright lamps burning—to attain enlightenment by constantly practicing the Path and maintaining a vegetarian diet, by serving at all kinds of meritorious duties. If contemplating mind subsumes all the various practices, it must have been empty and false when Buddha spoke of such things.

Bodhidharma answered: There are infinite skillful means in the scriptures that Buddha preached. Sentient beings have dull faculties: they are narrow and mean and do not understand very profound meanings. Therefore Buddha made temporary use of things involving contrived activities to represent the inner truth, which is without contrivance. If you do not cultivate inner practices, but just concentrate on external seeking, hoping to get blessings, it will not work.

When he talks of building monasteries, this means pure places. If you remove the three poisons forever and always purify the six sense faculties, so that body and mind are profoundly clear, and inner and outer are pure, this is "building a monastery."

As for "casting images," this refers to all the various provisional forms of enlightening practices cultivated by the sentient beings who seek the Path of enlightenment. It certainly does not mean that the wondrous true visage of the Tathāgata is something made out of cast metal. Therefore, those who seek liberation use their personal existence as the furnace, the Dharma as the fire, wisdom as the smith, and the three pure disciplines and the six perfections as the gold. They smelt and refine the enlightened identity of True Thusness within their bodies and pour it into all the molds of discipline, practicing according to the teaching until it is totally flawless and unstained: this naturally completes the true visage. What is called the ultimate eternally abiding subtle wondrous body of reality is not something contrived, something destructible. If people who seek enlightenment do not know how to cast the true visage, on what basis can they claim to have achieved meritorious acts?

As for "burning incense," this is not the worldly incense that has form: rather it is the incense of the uncontrived truth. It perfumes away defilements and cuts off the evil deeds of ignorance, making all evil karma dissipate. There are five kinds of incense of the True Dharma. First, the incense of discipline: being able to cut off all evil and cultivate all good. Second, the incense of stability: this means deep certainty in the Great Vehicle Mind, so there is no retrogressing. Third, the incense of wisdom: this means constant contemplation of body and mind, internal and external. Fourth, the incense of liberation: this means being able to cut off all the bonds of ignorance. Fifth, the incense of liberated perception: this means that awakened awareness is ever clear and reaches everywhere unobstructed.

These five kinds of incense are the supreme incense. No worldly kind can match them. When Buddha was in the world, he directed his disciples to take the fire of wisdom and light this priceless, precious incense to offer to all the buddhas of the ten directions. Nowadays sentient beings are foolish and have dull faculties: they take external fire to burn solid incense and hope for blessings and rewards. How can they get them?

"Scattering flowers" is also like this in meaning. It refers to the flowers of meritorious deeds of expounding the True Dharma for the benefit of sentient beings, sprinkling them with the water of the nature of True Thusness, and bestowing adornments on them all. Such meritorious deeds were acclaimed by the Buddha as ultimate and everlasting flowers that never fade and fall. If people scatter flowers like these, they get immeasurable blessings. The Tathāgata certainly did not direct his disciples to scatter flowers by cutting off blossoms and injuring plants. How do we know? Those who uphold pure discipline are not allowed to transgress against any of the myriad interwoven forms of heaven and earth. To take joy in injuring anything would incur great punishment. So much the worse for those today who seek blessings and rewards by destroying pure discipline and doing harm to beings. They want to gain, but they do harm—how could it be?

The "ever-bright lamp" is the mind of true enlightenment. Enlightened knowledge and clear comprehension are likened to a lamp. Therefore, all those seeking liberation always make their bodies the pedestal for the lamp, and their minds the bowl of the lamp, and faith the wick of the lamp; they add the various practices of discipline as the oil. The clear penetration of wisdom is likened to a lamp light constantly shining. This lamp of enlightenment shines through all the stupidity and darkness of ignorance. To be able to transmit this Dharma and open the way for awakening to it is "one lamp lighting hundreds and thousands of lamps." Since the lamp continues the light endlessly, it is called "the eternal light." In the past there was a buddha called Lamp Lighter—the meaning is similar.

Ignorant sentient beings do not understand what the Tathāgata said as skillful means: they concentrate on practicing false and contrived things that they cling to as attachments. Thus they light lamps of fresh worldly oil to light an empty room, and they say that they are abiding by the teachings. Isn't this wrong? What is the reason? From between his eyebrows Buddha emits a filament of light that illuminates eight thousand worlds in the ten directions. If the light of his body is fully revealed, it lights up everything in the ten directions. How can the use of these worldly lamps be considered beneficial? Upon examination of the principle of this, must it not be so?

"Constantly practicing the Path during the six time periods of the day" means to practice the Buddha Path constantly at all times amid the six senses. "Buddha" means "Enlightened One." To cultivate all enlightening practices in the moment, to tame the six senses so that the six sentiments are purified, to do this forever without abandoning it—this is called "constantly practicing the Path."

The "stupa" [to be "circumambulated"] is the body and mind. Let enlightened wisdom constantly patrol body and mind unceasingly from moment to moment. This is called "circumambulating the stupa." All of the sages of the past traveled this Path to find the bliss of *nirvāṇa*. Those who seek liberation today do not understand these principles: how can they be said to be practicing the Path? It seems that these days, those of dull faculties never engage in inner practices; they just cling to outer pursuits, using their material bodies to walk around worldly stupas, running around frantically day and night wearing themselves out in vain, with no benefit at all in regard to their true reality-nature. Those who are ignorant and deluded may truly be pitied!

As for "maintaining a vegetarian diet," we are always sure to meet those who do not comprehend the inner principle of this and who apply empty effort in vain. "Vegetarian diet" refers to evenness: it means carefully controlling body and mind and not letting them scatter in confusion. "Maintaining" means preserving. It means to preserve and maintain all the practices of discipline according to the Dharma. You must curb the six sentiments, control the three poisons, and scrupulously cultivate enlightened observation of the pure body and mind. Completely accomplishing [purity] in this sense can be called a "vegetarian diet."

Moreover, for those who maintain a vegetarian diet, there are five kinds of food. First, the food of joy in the Dharma, meaning to practice joyously the Tathāgata's True Dharma. Second, the food of the contentment of meditation: this means that inner and outer are clear and still, and body and mind are contented and happy. Third, the food of remembrance, meaning constant remembrance of all the buddhas, so that mind [mindful of Buddha] and mouth [reciting the buddha-name] are in accord. Fourth, the food of vows, meaning constant practice of vows of goodness when walking, standing, sitting, and lying down. Fifth, the food of liberation: this means that mind is always pure and unstained by worldly dusts. Maintaining a diet of the five pure foods is called a "vegetarian diet." If people say that they maintain a vegetarian diet, but they do not eat these five kinds of pure food, this is impossible.

There is fasting, "cutting off food." This means cutting off the food of the evil deeds of ignorance. As soon as you come in contact [with such evil deeds] it is called "breaking the fast." If the fast is broken, how can you get merit? There are deluded and foolish people in the world who do not understand the principle of this. They indulge body and mind and do evil deeds of greed and desire without shame, but when they cut off external foods they think they are maintaining a fast. They are like foolish children who see a rotting corpse: they say it's alive, but it surely is not.

"Serving" means always going by the Dharma. You must clearly understand the essence of truth within and transform the aspect of phenomena without. Inner truth cannot abandon phenomena: the storehouse of practices is there. If you understand this meaning, this is called "going by the Dharma." Serving implies respect and submission. It means respecting true reality-nature and subduing ignorance: this is called "serving." Because of respect, you do not dare to damage [the Dharma]. Because you are subdued, you do not let yourself indulge. If you can forever extinguish sentiments of evil and always preserve mindfulness of good, you are always serving, even if you do not show the signs of it. The signs of service are physical signs. In order to enable worldly, conventional people to show humility and subdue their minds, it is necessary to tame the external body and show signs that they will respect. [Such external signs of service] are shown when they are being used and hidden when they are put aside. Manifesting externals to illuminate the internal, they are in accord with reality-nature.

If you do not practice the Dharma of inner truth and just cling to external learning, then on the inside you are deluded and so give way to greed, anger, and ignorance, and always commit evil deeds; on the outside, you vainly manifest physical signs, but how can this be called service? Since you have no shame before the sages, you deceive the ordinary people. You will not avoid revolving down [into lower planes of existence]. How can you accomplish meritorious deeds? Since you achieve nothing, how will you seek the Path?

Huike also asked: In the *Warm Room Sūtra* it says that the congregation gains immeasurable merit by washing. How should we serve the Dharma so that merit is achieved? How can we accord [with reality] by just contemplating mind?

Bodhidharma answered: When "the congregation washes," this does not refer to any contrived worldly doings. The World Honored One expounded the *Warm Room Sūtra* at that time for his disciples so that they could receive his teaching on washing. Thus he made temporary use of worldly things as metaphors for the true principles and spoke in a veiled way about seven forms of meritorious deeds to be offered up. If all sentient beings use these seven washing methods to adorn them-

selves, they will be able to eliminate the three poisons
and remove the defilements of ignorance.

The seven are as follows: First, pure water: washing
clean with pure discipline is like pure water cleansing
away all dusts and defilements. Second, fire: contemplating inner and outer by means of wisdom is like fire that
can heat up the pure water. Third, a dipper: picking out
all forms of evil and getting rid of them is like a bath
dipper that can clear away the dirt and grease [from the
bathwater]. Fourth, willow branches: truly cutting off
all false words is like [scourging with] willow branches
that can dissipate an angry mood. Fifth, pure powder:
correct faith resolves doubts and leaves no worries, as
pure powder rubbed on the body can prevent disease.
Sixth, unguents: tempering the breath until it is supple
and soft and subduing all forms of hardness are like
spreading unguent all over the skin to moisten it. Seventh, clothing: shame and repentance toward all forms of
evil deeds are like a garment covering one's ugly form.

The foregoing seven items are a repository for secret
meanings in the *sūtra*. The Tathāgata at that time expounded them for those who have sharp faculties for the
Great Vehicle: they were not spoken for ordinary adher-
ents of the lesser vehicles whose knowledge is shallow
and inferior. These days no one can understand. The
"warm room" is the body. Therefore, light the fire of
wisdom and heat up the water of pure discipline to wash
clean the enlightened identity of True Thusness that is
within the body. Receive and uphold these seven methods
in order to adorn yourself.

At the time [Buddha spoke] the monks who were

intelligent all understood his meaning. They practiced as he had explained, and when the accomplished merit was complete, they all experienced the fruit of sagehood. These days sentient beings are stupid and their faculties are dull, and no one can fathom such things. They use worldly water to wash their physical bodies and think they are abiding by the teachings. Is this not a mistake? The enlightened identity, True Thusness, is fundamentally formless—it is not the ordinary physical form with its afflictions and defilements. How can you cleanse the body of ignorance with material water? If what you do is not in accord [with reality], how will you awaken to the Path? If you think that the material body attains purity, constantly contemplate this body. It is basically something born from lust and impurity. It is filled with filth and blocked off inside and out. If you seek purity by washing this body, it is like washing mud—it will never get clean. By such proof we clearly realize that external washing was not what the Buddha was talking about.

Huike also asked: According to what the *sūtra*s say, if we make our minds intent on remembrance of buddha by reciting the buddha-name, we are sure to find rebirth in the Pure Land in the West. By this wondrous gate we are sure to become enlightened. Why contemplate mind to seek libration?

Bodhidharma answered: Remembrance of buddha requires the cultivation of correct mindfulness. Comprehending the truth is correct; not comprehending it is wrong. With correct mindfulness you are sure to find the Western Paradise. If mindfulness is wrong, how can you get there?

"Buddha" means "the Enlightened One." It means enlightened observation of body and mind that does not let evil arise. [In reciting the buddha-name] "reciting" means "remembrance." It means remembering to uphold the practice of discipline and not forgetting energetic application. Completely comprehending this truth is called "correct mindfulness." Thus we know that remembrance by reciting is a matter of mind, not a matter of words. We use the trap to catch the fish: when the fish is caught we forget the trap. We use the words to get the meaning: when the meaning is gotten we forget the words.

If you adopt the words "reciting the buddha-name," you must practice the substance of reciting the buddha-name. If your recitation-remembrance has no real substance and your mouth just chants empty words in vain endeavor, what good will it do? Chanting and recitation-remembrance are far apart in names and meaning. Chanting is in the mouth; remembrance is in the mind. Thus we know that remembrance arises from mind, and it is called a gate to enlightening practice. Chanting is in the mouth, and is a form of sound. Seeking merit by clinging to form will never work. Thus the *sūtra* says: "All forms are empty and false." It also says: "To see the self by means of form, to seek the self by means of sound —such a person is traveling the wrong path and cannot see the Tathāgata." Contemplating in these terms, we know that the form of things is not true form.

Therefore we know that the meritorious deeds cultivated by all the sages of the past do not refer to external things: they all have to do with mind. Mind is the source of all the sages, and the master of the myriad evils. The eternal bliss of *nirvāna* is born from inherent mind. Mind is the gate for transcending the world, and the passageway to liberation. The one who knows the gate does not worry that it will be hard to succeed; the one who knows the passageway is not concerned about not arriving.

I think that these days people of shallow knowledge only recognize formalistic acts as meritorious works. They squander a lot of wealth presiding over many ceremonies for the dead and vainly having images and stupas constructed. To no purpose they put people to work constructing buildings and embellishing them. Wholeheartedly they use all their strength damaging themselves and deluding others, without ever knowing shame. When have they ever awakened? When they see contrived activities, they apply themselves scrupulously and become fondly attached to them. When we speak of formlessness, they look stupid and seem lost. What is more, they crave the minor pleasures of the world and are unaware of the great suffering to come. Those who "cultivate the Path" like this are wearing themselves out in vain—they have turned their backs on the straight and given their allegiance to the crooked, seeking merit with lying words.

Just manage to gather in mind. Reflect within and contemplate the eternal illumination. Cut off the mentalities of the three poisons: make them fade away and stop forever. Close the doors to the six thieves: do not let them cause disturbance. One by one perfect all the countless merits, the many kinds of adornments, and the measureless Dharma Gates. Transcend the ordinary and experience sagehood. What is right before your eyes is not far. Enlightenment is instantaneous—why wait for white hair?

The profound secrets of the gate of reality can hardly be related in full. This is an outline account of a small portion of the details of contemplating mind.

Treatise on the True Sudden Enlightenment School of the Great Vehicle, Which Opens Up Mind and Reveals Reality-Nature

THE GREAT PATH is fused with Mind, revealing the true pattern of reality. All the worthy sages past and future tend toward this gate. For those who awaken, the triple world is only mind. Those who do not awaken create dreams as they sleep. The School of the Great Vehicle must deal with forms and reveal the real. Those who completely awaken know that all phenomena are peaceful and still, that causal connections produce events, and that temporary combinations give rise to names. Those who do not comprehend become attached to names and abide in words, grasp concepts and run around misguided.

If you want to rein in the false and return to the real, so that defilement and purity are equalized, you must focus your attention and contemplate the self-revealed meaning of the mind's fundamental enlightenment. When your contemplation has power, you are still not beyond this meaning: mindfulness reaches the Other Shore and you are constantly in the deepest meditative concentration. If you practice this for a long time without stopping, naturally everything will be accomplished.

If you have concerns in your contemplation, gradually let your body and mind go toward the real. Empty out what is in your breast, so that all doings are forever stilled. Aware [of things] without giving them forms, you move freely in *samādhi*, closely nurturing the Path and its power. By this means you achieve the *dharmakāya*, the body of reality.

When you turn back and awaken to the mind source, there are no hindrances and no obstructions. Its body is like empty space, so it is called boundless *samādhi*. Mind has no going out or coming in, so it is called the *samādhi* of stillness. Amid all being it is pure and without seeking, so it is called inconceivable *samādhi*. *Samādhi* is undimmed and does not follow causal origination, so it is called the *samādhi* of the real nature of things.

Students are all seeking interpretive understanding: they do not seek direct experience. If you want to cultivate the Great Vehicle without knowing how to pacify mind, your knowledge is sure to go wrong.

There was a layman named Li Huiguang, a man of Changan in Yongzhou: his *dharma* name was Great Awareness. He paid no attention to glory or profit, but was intent on seeking enlightenment. He had served Huian and later on Shenhui. He received oral instructions personally from both of them and was given the gist of their teaching. He became able to reach the root and fathom the source of refined truths and subtle prin-

ciples: he appeared amid being and entered into nothingness in perfect fusion and freedom.

When not engaged in Chan contemplation, Layman
Li lamented that the multitudes were deluded, so he
published these Dharma essentials, revealing the abstruse
gate of phenomena and inner truth and displaying subtle
truths. This [treatise] could be called a boat for crossing
the seas directly to enlightenment. These words are trustworthy and true. He hoped that the unenlightened would
find enlightenment, that those not at peace would find
peace, and that those not yet liberated would find liberation.

Question: The Buddha Dharma is abstruse and mysterious, unfathomable to ordinary people. Its literature
is vast, its meanings hard to understand. May we inquire
about the Chan Master's essential teachings? Let us have
some provisional words, some expedient means, a direct
approach through direct words without secrets, that does
not abandon us worldly types.

Chan Master Great Awareness answered: Excellent!
Excellent! Observing your question, [I see that] your
basis as a bodhisattva is about to become pure and ripe.
I am forty-five and it has been more than twenty years
since I entered the Path, and there has never been anyone
who has asked about this.

What concerns do you have? What doubts are you
trying to resolve? Speak directly—there's no time to
bother with words.

Questioner: If we wish to enter the Path, what
Dharma should we practice, what Dharma should we
study, what Dharma do we seek, what Dharma do we

experience, what Dharma do we attain, in order to proceed toward enlightenment?

Answer: No Dharma is studied, and there is no seeking. No Dharma is experienced, and there is no attaining. No Dharma is awakened to, and there is no Path that can be cultivated. This is enlightenment.

Question: Since time without beginning we have been flowing along with birth and death at odds with inner truth. Having just heard the sudden teaching, we are confused and do not understand; our consciousness is dimmed and we do not know where we are. We are like drunks who cannot yet wake up sober. We humbly hope that you will extend yourselves down toward the deluded multitudes and bestow [some teachings] on those of little learning, so that by your skillful means we may meet with reality. What is our true identity?

Answer: It does not give rise to [false states of] mind: it is forever formless and pure.

Question: What is self-identity?

Answer: Seeing, hearing, knowing, the four elements, and all things each possess self-identity.

Question: From what is self-identity born?

Answer: It is born from false mind.

Question: How can one detach from self-identity?

Answer: When [false states of] mind do not arise, this is detachment.

Question: What is the Path? What is inner truth? What is mind?

Answer: Mind is the Path. Mind is inner truth. There is no inner truth outside mind and no mind outside inner truth. Since mind is capable of equanimity, it is called inner truth. Since inner truth is aware and can illuminate clearly, it is called mind. Since mind and inner truth are equal, it is called buddha. When mind finds this inner truth, you do not see birth and death: ordinary and sage are no different, objects and knowledge are not two, principle and phenomena are both fused, defiled and pure are one suchness. With true awareness according to inner truth, nothing is not the Path. Detached from self and other, you practice all practices at once. There is no before and after and no in between. Your bonds are untied and you are free: it is called the Path.

Question: How do we accord with inner truth to enter [into enlightenment]?

Answer: When you do not give rise to [false states of] mind and are forever formless, this is according.

Question: What is according with the Path?

Answer: A straightforward mind not attached to anything accords [with the Path].

Question: What is falsity?

Answer: Falsity is not knowing inherent mind.

Question: What is error?

Answer: Error is giving rise to all sorts of objects.

Question: What is inherent mind? What is false mind?

Answer: If you differentiate, it is false mind. If you do not differentiate, it is inherent mind.

Question: Where are they born from, the mind that differentiates and the mind that does not?

Answer: The mind that differentiates is born from error. The mind that does not differentiate is born from correct wisdom.

Question: Considered together, where are they born from?

Answer: There is nowhere they are born.

Question: If there is nowhere they are born, how can you say there is error or correct wisdom?

Answer: If you do not know inherent mind, you will proceed with all sorts of error. If you know inherent mind, this is correct wisdom.

Question: You just spoke of knowing and not knowing —what are these born from?

Answer: Knowing is born from awakening. Not knowing is born from false thinking.

Question: All sentient beings are in false thinking— how can they also be in correct wisdom?

Answer: All sentient beings are within correct wisdom —there is really no false thinking.

Question: Right now we are engaged in false thinking —how can we be said to have correct wisdom?

Answer: In reality, you are fundamentally without false thinking. When you call it false thinking, this is like a person drinking a potion that dilates the pupils, then looking for a needle in the sky: in the sky there is really no needle.

Question: Given that fundamentally false thinking does not exist, what are all today's practitioners trying to cut off in order to seek the Path?

Answer: Nothing is cut off and there is no path that can be sought.

Question: If there is no path to be sought and nothing to be cut off, then why in the scriptures did the World Honored One speak of cutting off false thinking?

Answer: In reality the World Honored One did not teach cutting off false thinking. As for cutting off false thinking: without detaching from false thinking, all sentient beings falsely feel that there is something attained and something cut off; they falsely perceive that the phenomena of false thinking exist. Following the concepts of sentient beings, the World Honored One spoke provisionally in terms of the phenomena of false thinking. In reality, he did not speak a word of it. He was like a good doctor prescribing medicine for a disease. If there is no disease, he does not prescribe medicine.

Question: If the World Honored One did not speak of false thinking, then who created false thinking?

Answer: Sentient beings themselves create it.

Question: Why do they not create correct wisdom, but go on perversely creating false thinking?

Answer: They do not know correct wisdom, so they have false thinking. If they knew correct wisdom, there would be no false thinking.

Question: If there is correct wisdom, there must be false thinking. How can you say there is no false thinking?

Answer: In reality, sentient beings have neither false thinking nor correct wisdom. Neither can be found.

Question: If both of them are unattainable, then it must be that neither ordinary people nor sages exist.

Answer: There are ordinary people and there are sages too, but you yourself do not know them.

Question: What is an ordinary person? What is a sage?

Answer: If you differentiate, you are an ordinary person. If you do not differentiate, you are a sage.

Question: Those who differentiate are ordinary, those who do not are sage. What about an infant, which does not differentiate? Can it be a sage?

Answer: If you adopt this interpretation, you are very foolish. Infants and children do not know good and bad, just as ignorant people do not recognize what is honorable and what is not. How could this be "not differentiating"? What is necessary is always to operate the differentiating mind within the inner truth of True Thusness, to attain nondifferentiating wisdom.

Question: Is no birth equivalent to nondifferentiating wisdom?

Answer: Observe for a while. Observe pure mind. Observe [states of] mind arising. You must perceive that mind has been pure from the beginning, not stained by external objects. With things and events, you must completely comprehend and see that [as products of] causes and conditions, no permanent identity can be found [for them]. Then you know that [the products of] causes and conditions are both empty and not empty. That is, worldly phenomena, all the profuse array of myriad images in the world, [conventional relationships like] lord and minister, father and mother, benevolence and righteousness, propriety and good faith—these are not destroyed [by the teaching of emptiness]. Therefore the scriptures give entry into *nirvāṇa* without destroying worldly phenomena. If you destroy the worldly *dharma*s, then you are an ordinary person flowing along with birth and death.

The phenomena of worldly causes and conditions have no independent existence. Being temporary combinations of causal factors, their essential identity is empty and ultimately cannot be found. Seeing this inner truth is called seeing reality-nature. Then, amid differentiation you find nondifferentiating wisdom. You always practice differentiating, yet without differentiating. This is "not destroying worldly phenomena." Thus the *sūtra* says: "Distinguish all causal connections and forms as entering into supreme reality without moving." Those who can awaken to this thereby have stillness right within movement.

Question: In the *Vimalakīrti Sūtra* it says: "He always sought the wisdom of having no thoughts and contemplating reality. Toward worldly phenomena, he reduced desires and knew satisfaction. As for the world-transcending Dharma, he sought it tirelessly. Without spoiling his dignified outward conduct, he was able to adapt to conventional ways while arousing the wisdom of spiritual powers, in order to guide sentient beings." What is the meaning of this?

Answer: The meaning of this is experienced by all the buddhas of past, present, and future: it is unfathomable to the intellect.

Question: Since "he always sought the wisdom of having no thoughts and contemplating reality," why do the scriptures talk of charity and discipline and the merits of humans and gods? Aren't these methods that involve thought? Why the discrepancy to make students doubt and not believe?

Answer: You all believe in things you do not understand. When Buddha spoke of charity and discipline and the merits of humans and gods, it was for the sake of sentient beings who are often immersed in false thinking. With immeasurable skillful expedient means, Buddha followed the mentality of sentient beings and preached in terms of false concepts to lead them to the gate of the Great Vehicle. If you do not believe me now, I will cite scriptures for you as proof. The *Lotus Sūtra* says: "These teachings of mine were adapted to sentient beings. The Great Vehicle is the basis." It also says: "In all the buddha-lands in the ten directions, there is only the Dharma of the One Vehicle. We use provisional names temporarily in order to guide sentient beings, but sentient beings have never been delivered by the lesser vehicles." It also says: "Do not approach the scholars of the canon of the lesser vehicles." It also says: "Only this one thing [the Buddha Vehicle] is real: the others are not." Moreover, the *All Things Are Uncompounded Sūtra* says: "If a person distinguishes discipline as a separate entity, he has no discipline. If he sees himself as having discipline, he has lost discipline."

On the basis of these quotes, it is obvious that Buddha expounded the Ultimate Gate. It is not that he said there is no [such thing as] human merit, but [when he did] he was just leading on sentient beings to enable them to enter buddha-wisdom. When the sages of the past and present speak of mind attaining mastery, of mind finding liberation, of mind achieving sagehood, this is the enlightened ones of past, present, and future sealing and settling your doubts.

Question: Buddha expounded the teaching of the One Vehicle to transform sentient beings. Now we all understand this. But what need was there to go on talking and confuse sentient beings? Wasn't it wrong?

Answer: You should not think this. The buddhas acted for sentient beings out of great compassion. Since many fall into the three evil paths [as hell beings, hungry ghosts, or animals], the buddhas open up the gate of expedient means and expound for them the six *pāramitā*s. Practicing giving, discipline, and patient endurance lets them get beyond the three evil paths. For those coming and going in the planes of humans and gods, practicing energetic progress, meditative concentration, and wisdom enables them to detach from the sufferings of birth and death, so that in the future they become enlightened.

Question: Did the buddhas of the past expound the Three Vehicles? Do the buddhas of the present expound the Three Vehicles?

Answer: The buddhas of past, present, and future all expound them.

Question: By what truth can we know this?

Answer: The *Lotus Sūtra* says: "If I now were to extol the Buddha Vehicle, sentient beings sunk in suffering would be unable to believe this teaching, and for violating it they would fall into the three evil paths. I would rather not expound the Dharma, but quickly enter *nirvāṇa*. Mindful of the power of the expedient means practiced by the buddhas of the past, for the Path I have attained, right now I too must expound the Three Vehicles." So we clearly know that all the buddhas of the past expounded the Three Vehicles in order to guide sentient beings to the One Vehicle.

Question: What is the One Vehicle?

Answer: Mind is the One Vehicle.

Question: How do we know that mind is the One Vehicle?

Answer: It is obvious that mind, which is empty and without anything there, is the One Vehicle.

Question: Do we become sages by completely perceiving that mind, being empty and without anything there, is the One Vehicle?

Answer: Yes, we become sages.

Question: Is the ordinary still there?

Answer: The ordinary is still there too.

Question: Are ordinary and sage different or not?

Answer: There is no difference at all. With awakening, the person who is ordinary in the morning is a sage by evening. Without awakening, you are subject to birth in the six planes of existence.

Question: What is this awakening you mention?

Answer: Awakening to mind.

Question: Are ordinary mind and sage mind one thing or two?

Answer: They are one.

Question: How can they be one?

Answer: If you completely perceive that reality-nature is pure and clean and from the beginning free from defilements and attachments, then you will know they are one.

Question: Who knows that there are no defilements or attachments?

Answer: Mind knows that there are no defilements.

Question: How does mind know that there are no defilements?

Answer: All the buddhas of past, present, and future explain that mind is formless and its essential being is ultimately unattainable. Thus we know that it has no defilements.

Question: Since it is formless, how can we know it has no defilements?

Answer: We know it has no defilements precisely because it is formless. If it had form or aspect or location, it would have defilements.

Question: You have spoken of mind. How many kinds of mind are there in all?

Answer: If you awaken, one mind that is unattainable. If you do not awaken, then there are many kinds of mind, an incalculable number.

Question: What is ordinary mind? What is sage mind?

Answer: If you grasp form, this is ordinary mind. If you detach from form, this is sage mind.

Question: Please instruct us in the essentials of mind that grasps form and mind that does not grasp form.

Answer: When those cultivating the Path have views of mind coming and going, views of mind being long or short, views of good and evil, hateful views and loving views, angry views and joyful views, views of right and wrong, views of ordinary and sage, views of independence and dependence, views of *nirvāṇa*, views of being liberated and of not being liberated, views of buddhas and bodhisattvas, views of meditative concentration, views of wisdom, and so on—all of these are [instances of] the mind of false thinking of ordinary people.

Question: What is the mind of people who are sages?

Answer: Not arousing a thought, not seeing a thing— this is the mind of the sages.

Question: Chan Master, have you attained the mind of the sages?

Answer: I have no attainment.

Question: If you have no attainment, how do you have knowledge?

Answer: Right now I have neither attainment nor knowledge. Thus the *sūtra* says: "He has no knowledge and no attainment. By having no attainment, he is a bodhisattva."

Question: Ultimately to whom does this truth belong?

Answer: It belongs to nothing at all. If it belonged to anything, this would be [more] revolving in birth and death. Since there is nothing to which it belongs, ultimately it abides forever.

Question: [We hear that] all sentient beings revolve with the eight consciousnesses and so do not find freedom. What are the eight consciousnesses?

Answer: They are [the consciousnesses] of eye, ear, nose, tongue, body, conceptual mind, [the synthesizing, evaluative, volitional, motivational complex, called] *manas*, and [the storehouse of all states of mind, called] *ālaya*.

"Consciousness" has the meaning of understanding and distinguishing. For example, when the eye interacts with form, the conceptual consciousness distinguishes this and may judge it to be good or bad. According to this judgment, form is engendered which influences the seventh consciousness, *manas*. Receiving this influence, [*manas*] grasps [at form] and transmits the influence to the seeds of all [potential] actions, which are already assembled in the eighth consciousness, called the storehouse. The eye-consciousness is this way, and so are the others.

The deeds done and the rewards received by all sentient beings first transform the storehouse consciousness into a causal basis for creating future actions. Thereby do causal bases rest upon each other one after another, and a succession of results proceeds unbroken. In the end the sentient beings return to the six paths and receive the sufferings of birth and death. Therefore, those who cannot completely comprehend mind are thrown into confusion by the eight consciousnesses.

These eight consciousnesses could be thought of as fundamentally present, or they could be said to create contrived activities on the basis of present causal connections. When causal connections join, it will engender future causal bases for action. If we want to cut them off and remove them now, and not let them be born, we must contemplate them correctly. Completely comprehend where the eye-consciousness comes from. Does it come from form? Does it come from the eye? Does it come from mind? If it comes from mind, since blind people have mind, why can't they produce eye-consciousness? If it comes from the eye, since dead people have eyes, why can't they distinguish form? If it comes from form, form is inert and unknowing [and cannot produce eye-consciousness]. None of these three causal links can act alone.

When you completely comprehend mind, you will know that when the eye sees form, the causal factor "the eye" is empty. Since the causal factor "eye" is empty, "form" is also empty. When you comprehend that "eye," "seeing," and "form" are all essentially empty, then there is no differentiation. Since there is no differentiation, the conceptual consciousness distinguishes without discriminating, and the seventh consciousness has no desire to grasp and no object to be grasped. Then in the storehouse of the eighth consciousness there are no more influences developing the seeds of impurity and defilement. Without these seeds, you are no more subject to birth and death: you abide forever in profound clarity, not born by birth or destroyed by destruction.

Question: The Buddha has three bodies—how are they attained?

Answer: The three bodies of Buddha are attained from the eight consciousnesses, by transforming the eight consciousnesses into the four wisdoms. When you reach these four wisdoms, you soon achieve the three bodies. Proceeding from cause to effect, we distinguish the three bodies like this. The five consciousnesses of eye, ear, nose, tongue, and body become the subtle observing wisdom. The sixth consciousness, the conceptual consciousness, becomes the accomplishment of action wisdom. The seventh consciousness, *manas*, becomes the wisdom of inherent equality. The eighth consciousness, *ālaya*, becomes the great mirror wisdom.

Question: What is the meaning of the "four wisdoms" that you can make this statement?

Answer: The first five consciousnesses are also called the five sense faculties. In this case the five sense faculties are the gates of wisdom through which wisdom is aware of the objects present, but without any falsity or defilement. Thus we take these five consciousnesses and make them into subtle observing wisdom. The sixth consciousness is also called the conceptual mind faculty. Here in the gate of wisdom we must work intently on awakening. Awakening means purity, and accord with the Dharma. With the real and the conventional equally in view, we perfect wisdom, transforming the conceptual mind into wisdom. Wisdom's awareness is able to know clearly without differentiating, and transform knowledge into wisdom. This is called the accomplishment of action wisdom. When *manas*, the seventh consciousness, has no grasping, it naturally has no hate or love. Since there is no hate or love, all things are equalized. Thus it is called the wisdom of inherent equality. As for *ālaya*, the eighth consciousness: when it is empty in the storehouse, defiled seeds are all pure. It is like a clear mirror hung in space. All the myriad images appear in it, but this bright mirror never thinks, "I can make images appear," nor do the images say, "We are born from the mirror." Since there is neither subject nor object, we call this wisdom the great mirror wisdom.

Question: If the four wisdoms are this way, what about the three bodies?

Answer: The great mirror wisdom is taken as the

dharmakāya, the body of reality. The wisdom of inherent equality is taken as the *saṃbhogakāya,* the reward body. The accomplishment of action wisdom and the subtle observing wisdom are taken as the *nirmāṇakāya,* the physical manifestation, the transformation body.

Question: How do you know it to be so?

Answer: We say that the greater mirror wisdom is taken as the body of reality because it is fully equipped with all stainless virtues, round and full with complete truth: it is like a worldly mirror that can show diverse images without differentiating.

The wisdom of inherent equality is taken as the reward body because when false mind is totally exhausted, everywhere-equal reality-nature is achieved and the myriad practices are perfected.

Accomplishment of action wisdom and subtle observing wisdom are taken as the transformation body because when the six sense faculties are stainless, you deliver sentient beings on a wide scale, detached from self and other, letting them share in your understanding and cultivate a basis [for enlightenment].

Question: Which among the three bodies of Buddha should sentient beings first cultivate?

Answer: The *sūtra* says: "From the everywhere-equal body of reality flows forth the reward body. From the reward body flows forth the body of transformation. From this transformation body flows forth the twelve-part teaching of the canon." Therefore, first cultivate the body of reality. When we say "body of reality" we mean the correct contemplation of the middle path between wondrous being and wondrous nothingness. If you awaken to this inner truth, this is the body of reality. By perceiving the body of reality, you find out that your own body and mind have always been at odds with reality. When you have seen the body of reality, you must work hard and intently until the worldly side naturally becomes pure and clean and harmonizes with Thusness. After a long time with Thusness, there is no thought of Thusness. When you have achieved this, this is the reward body. Thus, the body of reality is inherently present, but the body of reward is through cultivated practice. As for the transformation body, the *sūtras* say Buddha manifests all kinds of bodies called transformation bodies.

Question: If the three bodies are this way, what about the three jewels?

Answer: The three bodies of Buddha are also called the three jewels: that is, the jewel of the Buddha, the jewel of the Dharma, and the jewel of the Saṃgha.

Question: How many kinds of the three jewels are there?

Answer: Giving a full account, there are three kinds.

Question: What are they?

Answer: There are the three jewels of the one essence, the three jewels of differentiated aspects, and the three jewels of abiding and upholding.

Question: What are the three jewels of the one essence?

Answer: The purity of the enlightened nature of the essential body of true mind is called the jewel of the Buddha. Being round and full and complete with truth and equipped with countless meritorious functions is called the jewel of the Dharma. The oneness of the meritorious functions is the jewel of the Saṃgha.

Question: What are the three jewels of differentiated aspects?

Answer: "Differentiated aspects" means that this body of one's own is called the jewel of the Buddha. Being able to bestow happiness according to potentials and being willing to cultivate practice oneself is called the jewel of the Dharma. The four elements and the five clusters joining together without being at odds is called the jewel of the Saṃgha.

Question: What are the jewels of abiding and upholding?

Answer: Being good at supporting those above and making contact with those below, so that everything is pure and even, is called the jewel of the Buddha. Preaching according to people's mentalities, so that those who hear are full of joy, is called the jewel of the Dharma. Living in the community so that no conduct violates proper expedient means, and being able to harmonize everyone so there is no contention, is called the jewel of the Saṃgha.

Question: Why are they called jewels?

Answer: In the first place, they are neither inside nor outside nor in between. They are measureless and priceless. Metaphorically they are called the three jewels. If they had a price, they would not be called jewels. This is what is meant by the expression "priceless precious wish-fulfilling jewels."

Question: The *Lao Zi* says: "The Buddha Path has no [contrived] action, but there is nothing it does not do." What does this mean?

Answer: The Buddha Path is fundamentally and inherently without contrived activity. There is contrived activity because sentient beings create self-centered views as big as Sumeru. The true meaning of this is not something the conceptual mind can fathom. Only those who experience it can fully understand. Just manage to accomplish the work, and at a certain time there will be great awakening.

Question: The *sūtra* says: "All things come forth from this scripture." [What does this mean?]

Answer: [Here] "scripture" means mind. Mind can manifest everything. All people who practice develop illumination by cultivating the supreme correct path of unobstructed perfect awareness. All the buddhas, all the *tathāgatas*, begin with their own cultivation and end by transforming other beings. There is nothing that they do not achieve. Hence the saying "All things come forth from this scripture."

Question: The *sūtra* talks about the Tathāgata bearing the load. What does this mean?

Answer: You should just reflect back on reality-nature. Not abiding in your usual state, instead you become aware that you have no [permanent] body. Who will bear the load? Profoundly comprehending transcendent wisdom and broadly expounding it for people is bearing the load of the True Dharma. [The buddhas] convey its excellent meanings and let all sentient beings achieve meritorious deeds. Hence the talk of the Tathāgata bearing the load.

Question: What does it mean when the *sūtra*s say that the Tathāgata delivers sentient beings?

Answer: You must understand for yourself that the true identity of sentient beings is fundamentally pure, but when the six sense faculties create the vexations of form, sickness is born. When we observe that birth is fundamentally empty, what is there that can be delivered? Therefore, if you say that the Tathāgata delivers beings, you are attached to [notions of] self and others and beings.

Question: What is the meaning of "diamond *prajñā-pāramitā*"?

Answer: "Diamond" is the mind of form. *Prajñā* is purity. *Pāramitā* means reaching the other shore.

Question: [What is the meaning of] "Not grasping at form, Thusness does not stir"?

Answer: If your mind creates [notions that] there is coming and going, that is, contrived phenomena, all of these are forms of unrest. If your mind does not create them, there is no coming or going: amid uncontrived phenomena, there is detachment from both moving and not moving. This is permant abiding. Thus it is said: "Thusness does not stir."

Question: The *Warm Room Sūtra* says that by washing with the seven things, the monks get merit without measure. Please tell us the meaning of this merit.

Answer: What the *sūtra* says is quite true. If you have the seven things and wash with them, inner and outer are sure to be in accord, and the merit will be measureless.

If you always trifle with the reality-nature of mind, if you indulge greed and anger, if you wrangle over right and wrong, if you make other people groan and cry, then even if you wash with the seven things, you are shedding the Buddha's blood: you are constantly putting together the *karma* of the three mires. If you wash like this, it is like washing in mud. You must stop this completely. Let body and mind be pure. Do not arouse greed and anger, and naturally you will be equanimous and detach from discrimination. With the water of nondiscrimination, you wash away all the dust and filth and become fully pure and clean.

Question: How should we deal with this mind of the three poisons in order to achieve the six *pāramitās*?

Answer: You must be brave and bold and advance energetically. Toward the three poisons, take the three vows.

Vow to cut off all evils, to deal with the poison of anger. Vow to cultivate all forms of good, to deal with the poison of ignorance. Vow to deliver all sentient beings, to deal with the poison of greed. When the ability to cut off evil and the ability to cultivate good come together in the mind, the three poisons are curbed, and you achieve the three pure disciplines.

Next, let us explain subduing mind. Toward the five clusters [form, sensation, perception, motivational synthesis, and consciousness] we develop five kinds of subduing mind.

First, we vow to view all sentient beings as worthy sages and ourselves as ordinary people. Second, we vow to view all sentient beings as kings and ourselves as commoners. Third, we vow to view all sentient beings as teachers and ourselves as disciples. Fourth, we vow to view all sentient beings as parents and ourselves as children. Fifth, we vow to view all sentient beings as lords and ourselves as servants.

The six *pāramitā*s are also called the six deliverances: [they are] giving, discipline, patience, energetic progress, meditative concentration, and wisdom. These are used to deal with the six planes of existence. When the six sense faculties are pure, the six planes of existence are not born.

When you have no attachments to inner or outer, and you spontaneously give, this comprises *dānapāramitā*, the perfection of giving. When good and evil are equal, and neither can be found, this comprises *śīlapāramitā*, the perfection of discipline. When objects and knowledge are in harmony and no longer at odds, this comprises *kṣāntipāramitā*, the perfection of patience. When great stillness never stirs as the myriad practices are spontaneously so, this comprises *vīryapāramitā*, the perfection of energetic progress. When wondrous stillness flourishes and the body of reality spontaneously appears, this comprises *dhyānapāramitā*, the perfection of meditation. When wondrous stillness opens into illumination, changeless, eternally abiding, not attached to anything, this comprises *prajñāpāramitā*, the perfection of wisdom.

These are called the six *pāramitā*s. The Sanskrit word *pāramitā* means "reaching the other shore."

Question: Hitherto among conventional types, all the question-and-answer dialogues have been [attempts at] assessment that give rise to [states of false] mind and give birth to affliction. But you, Chan Master, have given us joy and left us without the slightest doubts. We do not dare to do as we wish [and question you further], fearing to trouble you.

Answer: If you have no doubt, do not force questions. If the Dharma had questions and answers, it would have high and low. Without questions or answers, the Dharma is everywhere equal. If you seek to extend your views and interpretations, you lose the fundamental Path, and it gives you the barrier of the knowledge you fashion in your mind. It makes waves arise in your mind. But if you really do have doubts and sticking points, you must diligently ask about them to test what is real.

Question: What does it mean when the *Laṅkāvatāra Sūtra* talks about being far removed from awareness and the objects of awareness?

Answer: When [such subject–object] awareness is not born, the mind is at peace and unshakable.

The questioner concludes: Though I am an ordinary layman, my consciousness has already entered the Path. What I hear the Master say now is all genuine supreme enlightenment. Intent on fulfilling his vows, his mind never retreats. Suddenly cutting off worldly entanglements, his mind's spirits and six consciousnesses are located nowhere—he is focused on the One Mind.

As we look up to him and thirst, we cannot stop ourselves from crying and groaning. He makes us know shame: we cannot hold back our sad tears. We feel regret deep in our hearts that for so many aeons we have in our delusion missed this truth. If it were not for the Chan Master being compassionate to us lowly ones, we would have no means by which we could awaken.

Therefore we are calling this "Treatise on Great Liberation." If writing this treatise is in accord with the intent of the sages, then let this blessing be revealed to all sentient beings alike. If it is not in accord with the intent of the sages, I hope the wrongdoing will be wiped away. If there are no people [worthy to do so], it should not be transmitted. I fear that it would be used to slander and attack the wisdom of the Dharma. If there are people of real awakening and sufficient merit to transmit it, let them share our deep compassion and care. The Dharma of the Great Path cannot be shown lightly. It does not allow exultation or disputation. It is just the mind in silence knowing for itself: false thoughts are not born, and the mentality of self and objects is extinct.

GLOSSARY

asura: See *six planes of existence*.

bodhi: Enlightenment; the perception of reality.

bodhisattva: Enlightening being. Bodhisattvas are those who remain active in the world after their enlightenment, using their enlightened perception to aid other beings toward enlightenment.

body of reality: See *buddha-bodies*.

buddha: In Great Vehicle Buddhism, everyone is (potentially) a buddha, an enlightened one—everyone has buddha-nature, a fundamentally enlightened true identity. More narrowly, buddhas are those who have actualized this enlightened identity, for example the Indian sage Śākyamuni, the historical Buddha.

buddha-bodies: Different aspects of the being of the buddhas are spoken of as the bodies of Buddha. Common usage defines three buddha-bodies: *dharmakāya* Buddha, the body of reality, buddhas as the inconceivable formless absolute, the one reality, the ground of all particular being; *nirmāṇakāya* Buddha, the transformation body, or emanation body, in which Buddha takes form and appears in the world to teach living beings; and *saṃbhogakāya* Buddha, the reward body, the body of enjoyment, experienced by bodhisattvas as the fruit of their practices, marked by supreme bliss and the ability to communicate bliss.

causal nexus: Buddhism sees all conditioned phenomena as products of complex interactions of cause and effect.

cessation and contemplation: Two complementary forms of meditation, as taught by Tiantai Buddhism. Cessation means stopping the deluded stream of consciousness; contemplation means observing the pattern of cause and effect and the ultimate true nature of phenomena.

clusters: See *skandhas*.

consciousness: Zen adopts the Yogacara Buddhist analysis of eight consciousnesses. The first five consciousnesses are those associated with the sense faculties of sight, hearing, taste, touch, and smell; the sixth consciousness is the conceptual faculty that distinguishes and classifies the data of experience; the seventh consciousness includes value judgments and hence motivations to action; the eighth consciousness, known as the storehouse consciousness, is the repository of all possible mental states, perceptions, and experiences. Zen practices are particularly directed toward purifying and transforming the sixth and seventh consciousnesses, which, conditioned by egoism and delusion, operate in ordinary people as barriers to enlightenment.

dharma: This word has different levels of meaning. All phenomena are *dharma*s—things, events, concepts. *Dharma* can also mean reality itself, and the teaching of reality. Buddha Dharma is both the teaching of enlightenment and the enlightenment taught—reality as perceived by buddhas.

four elements: In traditional thought, the constituents of all material things—fire, water, earth, and air.

Indra's Net: A metaphor used in Huayan Buddhism to illustrate the interpenetration of all realities. Picture a vast net with a jewel at every node: in every jewel appear the reflections of all the other jewels, which in turn each reflect the myriad images of all the other jewels, ad infinitum.

karma: Actions; deeds. According to Buddhist teaching, one's present life experience is the result of one's deeds in this and previous births.

Lao Zi: Old spelling: *Lao Tzu;* also called *Tao Te Ching.* Classic third century B.C.E. collection of Taoist aphorisms suggesting how self and society may be brought to harmony with the natural pattern.

nirvāṇa: Peaceful extinction; liberation from delusion. At the elementary level, this is seen as the antithesis of *saṃsāra,* the round of birth and death. For bodhisattvas, *nirvāṇa* and *saṃsāra* are one.

pāramitā: "Crossing to the other shore"—transcendence through the perfection of giving, discipline, patience, energetic progress, meditation, and wisdom: basic practices of the bodhisattva.

prajñā: Transcendent wisdom, free of subject–object dualism, that perceives reality.

pratyeka buddha: An isolated buddha, self-enlightened through contemplation of cause and effect, who does not appear in the world to teach others.

samādhi: Meditative concentration; focus on reality.

Samantabhadra: A bodhisattva whose name means "Universally Good." Buddha is often pictured flanked by Samantabhadra on his right, representing truth, and Mañjuśrī on his left, representing wisdom.

saṃsāra: Cyclic existence; birth and death.

six planes of existence: In the round of birth and death, beings may be born as hell beings, as hungry ghosts, as animals, as *asuras* (titanic demigods), as human beings, or as *devas* (celestial gods).

skandhas: The five clusters, or aggregates, that make up psychophysical existence: form, sensation, perception, motivational synthesis, and consciousness.

śrāvaka: "Hearer"—one who understands only the most elementary level of the Buddhist teaching; such a one sees *nirvāṇa* as the opposite of *saṃsāra* and clings to the experience of emptiness and cessation.

stupa: A memorial mound containing relics of a buddha, used as a focus of devotion, especially in popular Buddhism.

Suchness: See *Thusness*.

Sumeru: In Buddhist cosmology, the great polar mountain at the center of each world-system.

Tathāgata: An epithet of Buddha, "the one who has come from Thusness."

ten stages: The stages of a bodhisattva, as enumerated in the *Huayan Sūtra:* joy, stainlessness, the stage of emitting light, incandescent wisdom, the unsurpassable stage, the stage where reality appears before them, the far-going stage, the immovable stage, the stage of good wisdom, the stage where the bodhisattva emits clouds of Dharma.

three jewels: Buddha, the enlightened one; Dharma, the enlightening teaching; Saṃgha, the harmonious community of those cultivating the path of enlightenment.

Thusness: Also called True Thusness, or Suchness; reality itself, the real nature of all phenomena, eternal, unchanging, without falsity; synonymous with buddha-nature, *dharmakāya*, inherent pure mind, the womb of the *tathāgatas*, the realm of reality.

triple world: The realm of desire, the world as experienced by ordinary people under the influence of their desires; the realm of form, the world as observed in meditation, neutral form beyond desires; the formless realm, the most refined meditation states, infinite consciousness, infinite space, total nothingness, and the state that is neither thought nor no thought. Buddhas transcend the triple world.

vehicle: The Buddhist teaching is likened to a vehicle because it conveys sentient beings to enlightenment. The Two Vehicles are the Buddhism of the *śrāvaka*s and the *pratyeka*s, who do not realize the complete meaning. The Three Vehicles are these two plus the bodhisattva vehicle. The *Lotus Sūtra* teaches that the Three Vehicles are just temporary expedients: in reality there is only One Vehicle, the Buddha Vehicle, which aims to lead all sentient beings to develop enlightened perception.

Western Paradise: The Pure Land of Amitabha Buddha, the Buddha of Infinite Life and Infinite Light, a land of bliss and ease where the faithful are born by remembrance of Buddha through recitation of the buddha-name.

Zhuang Zi: The most profound book among the Chinese philosophical classics, composed around 300 B.C.E.; often read in Buddhist circles for its parallels with the Buddhist teaching. Old spelling: *Chuang Tzu.*